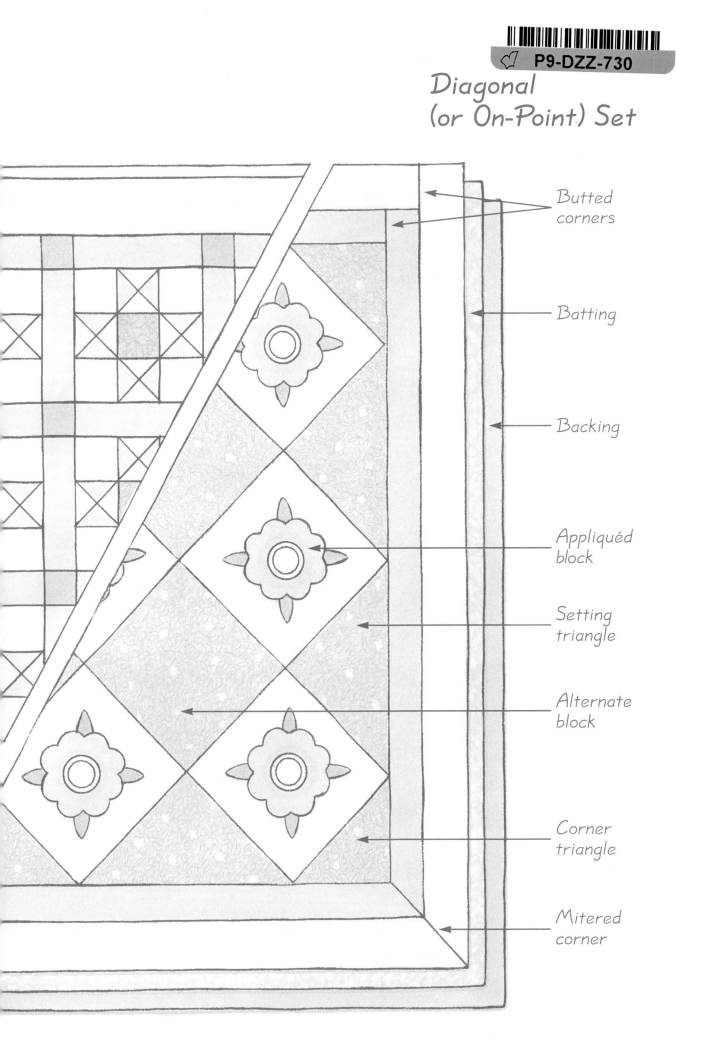

Diagonal (or On-Point) Set

Butted corners

Batting

Backing

Appliquéd block

Setting triangle

Alternate block

Corner triangle

Mitered corner

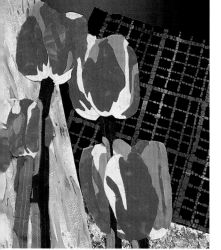

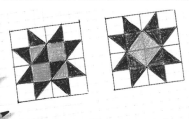
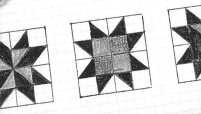

Rodale's Successful
Quilting Library®

Drafting
& Design
Simplified

Sarah Sacks Dunn
Editor

RODALE®

RODALE

WE **INSPIRE** AND **ENABLE** PEOPLE TO IMPROVE
THEIR LIVES AND THE WORLD AROUND THEM

Book Producer: Eleanor Levie,
    Craft Services, LLC
Editor: Sarah Sacks Dunn
Art Director: Lisa J. F. Palmer
Writers: Charlotte Warr Andersen,
    Karen Kay Buckley, Elsie M. Campbell,
    Karen Eckmeier, Gloria Hansen,
    Dixie Haywood, Claudia McGill,
    Darra Duffy Williamson, Joen Wolfrom
Photographer: John P. Hamel
Illustrator: Mario Ferro
Copy Editor: Erana Bumbardatore
Indexer: Nan N. Badgett
Hand Model: Melanie Sheridan

Rodale Inc.
Editorial Manager, Rodale's Successful
    Quilting Library: Ellen Pahl
Layout Designer: Keith Biery
Product Manager: Daniel Shields
Product Specialist: Jodi Schaffer
Series Designer: Sue Gettlin

We're always happy to hear from you.

For questions or comments concerning the editorial content of this book, please write to:

Rodale Inc.
Book Readers' Service
33 East Minor Street
Emmaus, PA 18098

Look for other Rodale books wherever books are sold. Or call us at (800) 848-4735.

For more information about Rodale and the books and magazines we publish, visit our Web site at:

www.rodale.com

On the cover: Friends Forever, by
    Karen Kay Buckley & Friends
On these pages: Sunset Wheel of Mystery, by
    Brooke Flynn
On the Contents pages: Sunset-at-Sea, by
    Mary Jane Cook

Library of Congress Cataloging-in-Publication Data published the first volume of this series as:

    Rodale's successful quilting library.
        p.   cm.
    Includes index.
    ISBN 0–87596–760–4 (hc: v. 1:alk paper)
    1. Quilting. 2. Patchwork. I. Soltys, Karen
Costello. II. Rodale Press.
TT835.R622 1997
746.46'041—dc21   96–51316

Drafting & Design Simplified:
    ISBN 1–57954–503–3 hardcover

**Distributed to the book trade
by St. Martin's Press**

2 4 6 8 10 9 7 5 3 1   hardcover

Contents

Introduction

Everything I ever needed to know about drafting quilting designs, I learned from my dad. Now, my dad's a chemist by profession, not a quilter, but he still taught me some very important lessons fairly early in life.

Lesson #1. Graph paper is cool. Dad used to have stacks of graph paper, torn out of partially used lab books, piled in his study at home. I remember it was tied with white thread at the fold; the blue squares were little compartments lined up, waiting for letters (one per box) or drawings (always on the lines, that's what they're for). I used to swipe it from his office and draw pictures on it for hours. I have some of that unused graph paper still, saved just as I save that "special" fabric that I know in my heart I'll never really cut up.

Lesson #2. Always have a sharp pencil point. When you're doing [insert your least favorite school subject here] homework, if your pencil point is dull, it smears and your writing is distorted, and you make mistakes. Dad wouldn't help us with homework until he had inspected our pencil points and found them satisfactorily sharp and precise. (See page 12.)

Lesson #3. Plan, plan, plan. Take the time up front to figure out what you're doing, and you'll do it right the first time. It takes way more time to redo a mistake than to plan carefully so you avoid the mistake in the first place. (This applies today to drafting for quiltmaking just as well as it did to fifth-grade models of the solar system.)

Those three things are really all that you need to know. That's it. Honest. The rest is pretty much just drawing—especially with the clear step-by-step instructions that accompany the techniques in this book. Forget your math phobia, your fear of equations, those flashbacks to the panic attacks you suffered in geometry class. Drafting stellar quilt patterns doesn't require you to be a math major—or even a whiz at numbers. With a few readily available tools, a calculator, the reference tables and charts at the back of this book, and a little inspiration, you can design, draft, and make the quilt of your dreams in the exact size you want, whether it's pieced, appliquéd, or a combination of techniques.

Where do you find inspiration? There's no end to sources. Flip through the pages of this book and you'll see where our experts get their ideas—books of classic quilt blocks, or books about art, design, and gardening. And don't forget calendars, museums, pictures, snapshots, and even items from nature that catch your eye. Once you find an image (or a portion of an image) that you like, you can play with it: Add or delete lines, repeat the image, or combine it with other elements, images, and motifs to make the design you really want. (See page 36 for a quick lesson in some design basics.)

And don't forget about your computer. The same tool you use to e-mail your quilting friends can quickly become your favorite quilting design tool. See page 48 for information on creating both patchwork and appliqué designs with specialized quilting software.

Then, make your block or design whatever size you want. With this book in hand, you no longer need to be dependent on commercial patterns in the size provided. Just because you can't find the particular block you want in the size you need for your parents' king-size anniversary quilt (surprise, Mom and Dad!), there's no need to abandon or change your idea. Use any one of the methods described on pages 14–17 to size the block so the quilt will fit the top of the bed exactly. And if you can't find exactly the right design? Create it yourself! Our dream team of quiltmaking experts—Charlotte Warr Andersen, Karen Kay Buckley, Elsie Campbell, Karen Eckmeier, Gloria Hansen, Dixie Haywood, Claudia McGill, Darra Duffy Williamson, and Joen Wolfrom—share the latest and greatest techniques for both drafting and design.

So dream no more of the "perfect" quilt design: Just draft it!

Sarah Sacks Dunn

Sarah Sacks Dunn
Editor

1 Always do your drafting work where you have good, bright light. This way, you will be able to see clearly the details you are drawing, and you will make fewer mistakes as a result.

2 Some of the most wonderful (and useful!) tools you will use when you are drafting quilt patterns are not found in quilt stores, but in office, art, or building supply stores. Look for drafting triangles, T-squares, erasers, mechanical pencils, compasses, protractors, and French curves. You'll really appreciate these tools once you begin drafting frequently.

3 If you've made a drafting mistake and can't erase or eliminate it, simply tape a clean piece of paper over the portion that's wrong. (For graph paper, keep the lines aligned.) Then rework just that portion, instead of redoing the entire design.

4 Turn your geometric or abstract design upside down or sideways. It may be stronger or more interesting, or you may like it better when viewed from a different angle.

5 Allow enough time to complete the drafting of an entire phase or part of your design in one sitting. Starting and stopping is distracting and sometimes leads to errors. On the other hand, if you run up against a problem you can't resolve, take a break and come back to it later.

6 While you're in the planning stages, ask a friend for input. Sometimes a fresh perspective, even one from a nonquilter, can lead to even better options.

7 If you don't have large paper handy, make your own oversize sheets of paper by adhering lengths of freezer paper together. Overlap the long edges by ½ inch and press them from the nonwaxy side with a hot, dry iron. Peel the larger sheet off your ironing surface carefully to maintain the overlapped bond.

8 Make a simple light table by turning a large, clear glass baking dish upside down over a string of white Christmas tree lights.

9 If you are using graph paper, check that its dimensions are accurate in both directions. Sometimes paper can stretch during printing, distorting the grid. Also keep in mind that the lines may be printed slightly darker on one side of the paper than the other (making them easier to follow) and that you may need a darker-than-usual setting on the photocopier if you want the grid lines to reproduce.

10 Draw with the side of your pencil lead rather than the tip to prevent it from becoming dull and widening the line being drawn.

11 Where precision is absolutely critical, avoid drafting with thick acrylic rulers. These can cast shadows, and their thickness can cause you to angle your pencil awkwardly, slightly affecting the accuracy of the drawn shape.

12 If your compass slips or your circles aren't perfect, try inserting an old cutting mat or a scrap piece of cardboard under your sheet of paper. This will hold the compass point in place and protect the other sheets of paper on your pad.

13 Keep your design simple. The more you try to include, the more complex and confusing your design will become. Modify a traditional block with just one or two changes, and limit the number of elements you really want to include in an appliqué design.

14 Keep a folder or notebook for inspiration. Create a record of ideas that appeal to you. You might take Polaroid photos or make photocopies. Then you can always browse through your notebook to get inspiration when planning your next quilt.

15 Before finalizing a design, check your fabric stash for exciting prints and visual textures. These may inspire you to delete lines and enlarge or combine pieces, so you can let the fabric convey the design elements.

16 Value (light versus dark) can make a big difference in the mood of your design. For excitement, use high contrast; for a more subdued effect, use low contrast.

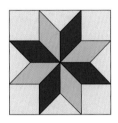

17 Adapt your patchwork and appliqué designs to use as quilting designs. Repeat the same motif, resized to fit a plain block, quiet space, border, or cornerstone. Alternatively, use a related motif, such as a quilted apple in the corners of an Apple Core patchwork quilt.

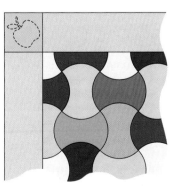

18 A flannel-backed plastic tablecloth makes a large and inexpensive design surface. It's also handy for transporting projects—just roll it up and everything stays in place. Purchase a spare tablecloth, and keep it packed along with your design tools.

19 Accompany that lovely gift quilt with a card that features a smaller drafting of the block, colored in. This is also great for those occasions when the quilt isn't quite finished in time; it lets the receiver know what's coming. Or use your computer to draft stationery or holiday cards that feature your latest quilt design.

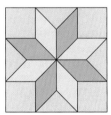

HAPPY ANNIVERSARY!

20 Inspiration for appliqué designs can turn up in unlikely places. Grocery store flyers have wonderful drawings of fruits and vegetables. Children's coloring books have line drawings that are easy to adapt. Note cards, postcards, and magnets found in gift shops may also contain simple, appealing graphics.

Every quilter knows how important accuracy is to the success of a quilt. We all focus a great deal of attention on having just the right tools for precise cutting, accurate piecing, and perfect pressing. Having the right tools for drafting is just as important. This will give you the best results from the start, which is especially critical when you're drafting and designing your own patterns. There's not a lot you'll need, and buying basic supplies won't break the bank. So equip yourself properly for the job, and you'll enjoy both the process and the results immensely.

Getting Ready

Accurate drafting doesn't require a lot of fancy gadgets. Good lighting; a large, flat work surface; a comfortable chair; and a few basic materials are all you really need to get started. Browse the notions department of your local quilt shop and the aisles of office, art, drafting, and architectural supply stores for quality drafting tools. Invest in the best that you can afford; don't shortchange yourself by trying to adapt what you have on hand for drafting. For the utmost in consistency and accuracy, use the same materials and tools—graph paper, brand of ruler, compass, pencil—throughout an entire project.

If you've abandoned paper and pencil for keyboard and mouse, there's an entire chapter devoted to you. See "Creating on the Computer" on page 48.

See "Creating on the Computer" on page 48.

What You'll Need

¼" graph paper

Unlined paper (newsprint or sketch paper)

Pencil with sharpener or mechanical pencil with .05 mm lead

Erasers

Rulers

Compass

Yardstick compass

Protractor

Calculator

Proportional scale

Template plastic

Optional:

    Isometric graph paper

    Colored pencils

    T-square or drafting triangle

Drafting Essentials

Paper

There are many kinds of paper appropriate for drafting quilt blocks, designs, or layouts. Quarter-inch (four squares per inch) graph paper helps you draw and evenly divide perfectly square blocks. An 8½ × 11-inch pad is fine for smaller blocks or designs; if your design is larger, look for oversize graph paper. Keep a pad of plain, unlined paper on hand for drafting nongrid-based blocks where preprinted lines might be distracting. For 60-degree shapes, such as equilateral triangles, hexagons, and diamonds, invest in a pad of isometric graph paper with rows of equilateral triangles.

Tip

For easy measuring, look for graph paper with the 1" increments (every fourth line) printed slightly darker.

TOOLS OF THE TRADE

11

Pencils & Erasers

You'll go through a lot of pencils (and erasers!) while drafting and drawing. Select a hard-lead pencil to draw clean, crisp, accurate lines; soft lead smears too easily. Have a sharpener on hand so you can keep your pencil point consistently sharp while you draft. Or use a mechanical pencil with a .05 mm lead, and you'll spend less time worrying about sharp points. Keep a rubber or gum eraser nearby to take care of those inevitable slips and mistakes. Colored pencils are great if you like to experiment with shadings and colorations.

Rulers

You'll find a dizzying variety of drafting rulers when you shop. In general, a thin metal drafting ruler with a non-slip cork back is ideal for precise drafting. Or choose a thin plastic or acrylic ruler with a beveled edge so it doesn't cast a shadow as you draw. **Be aware that your ruler might include "dead space" (an un-measured area) before the in-crement lines begin and that metric measurements might be marked along one edge.** Your clear acrylic rotary rulers are useful when you need perfectly perpendicular or parallel lines.

} **Dead space**

Compass

A compass with an adjustable span allows you to draw perfect circles and arcs. Make sure your compass in-cludes a threaded crossbar so it will hold the radius that you set.

If your compass is too small to draw a large enough circle or arc, adapt a yardstick to do so, using a nifty clip-on notion to make what's called a yardstick compass. (These are available at drafting and art supply shops.) **Measure along a second ruler to set the span to the exact radius you want,** and adjust as needed.

A protractor is a tool, usually semi-circular, that enables you to measure and mark angles. Use it to mark angles in a block of your own design, to mark off the "petals" in a Dresden Plate block, or to determine the number and width of the "blades" in a Grandmother's Fan. **Look for a translucent protractor that has a thin, easy-to-use baseline to line up with your drawing.**

Tip

Clear acrylic rotary rulers with 45° and 60° lines are also helpful for drafting and checking these common angles.

Keep a calculator close by for quick and accurate math. Use it in combination with a **proportional scale. This handy tool allows you to determine exactly how much to enlarge or reduce any patch, block, motif, or pictorial design** so it fits properly into your quilt design. Line up the measurement of the original design on the inside ring with the desired measurement on the outside ring. Look in the window opening to see the percentage to increase or reduce, then use that figure when multiplying the original dimensions on your calculator.

Tip

When photocopying or scanning, use the number shown in the window of the proportional scale and set the machine to that percentage.

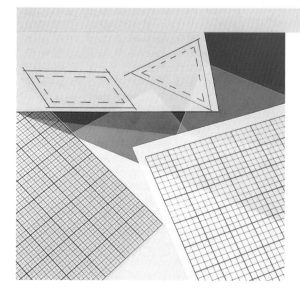

Some blocks are more easily made using traditional plastic templates (and some quilters prefer to use them for all their piecing). **Template plastic is available in a variety of colors, styles, and thicknesses.** Choose a slightly opaque plastic that is easy to mark with a sharp pencil or ultrafine permanent marker, or use a gridded variety that helps ensure accuracy when measuring. Avoid template plastic with a slick, slippery side; a template cut from such material will tend to slide on the fabric as you are tracing around it.

TOOLS OF THE TRADE

Pieced Blocks
in Any Size

Declare your independence! Learn how to draft patchwork patterns in any size you want from expert quilter Joen Wolfrom. You'll enjoy the freedom to create blocks that fit your project perfectly, and you can do it without fancy tools, math, or a calculator. In short, there's no easier way to resize a block than a time-honored method called the flexible grid. The rewards are great: an accurate grid to draw your selected pattern in the exact size you want, and a drafting skill that you'll use over and over again.

Getting Ready

Look through an encyclopedia or reference book of classic patchwork blocks. You will notice that most of the designs are blocks based on a square grid with the same number of divisions horizontally and vertically (2 × 2, 3 × 3, 4 × 4, 5 × 5, and so on). Choose a block to draft. If the grid is not apparent, see if you can draw lines on top of the block to divide it into sections that can be easily drawn and pieced.

Decide on the size you want to draft your chosen block. If the number of grid divisions divides easily into the block size, you can easily draw it on preprinted graph paper. Otherwise, follow along with the steps in this chapter to draft a sample Wedding Ring block. Then use the same process to draft your chosen pattern. You'll have this technique down pat after you draft just a few different blocks.

What You'll Need

Large white drawing paper

Mechanical pencil or lead pencil with a sharp point

Clear acrylic rulers

Drafting ruler

Colored pencils

Flexible Grid

1

To begin resizing your chosen block, you'll need to answer four questions:

1. What size do I want the *finished block* to be? (We'll choose 8 inches.)

2. How many horizontal and vertical *grid divisions* are there in my block? (Wedding Ring, pictured, has 5.)

3. What number is larger than the desired finished block size (the answer to #1) and can be divided evenly by the answer to #2? (Here, our answer is 10.) This is your *key number*.

4. What number do you get when you divide the number of grid divisions (#2) into the key number (#3)? (10 ÷ 5 = 2.) This is the *increment*.

 Tip

When you're answering question #3, use the smallest possible number. For instance, use 10 rather than 15 for a number that is evenly divisible by 5.

PIECED BLOCKS IN ANY SIZE

2

On a sheet of plain paper, draw a square the size of your desired finished block (in this case, 8 inches). **A large square acrylic ruler** is very helpful for drawing true 90-degree corners.

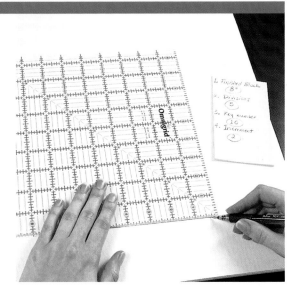

3

Place the 0 end of a drafting ruler near the bottom left corner of your square. Then angle the ruler to align the inch mark that is the key number (10, in our example) with the opposite side.

Using the increment number from question #4, make tick marks along the ruler at intervals the length of your increment. (Our answer was 2, so we'll make a mark every 2 inches.) **Mark at the 2-, 4-, 6-, and 8-inch lines on your ruler.** These tick marks divide the square into five equal sections.

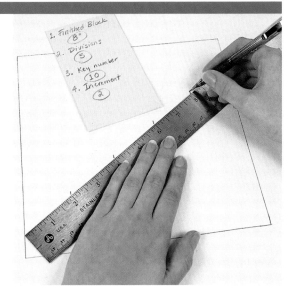

4

Draw vertical grid lines as follows: Align one side of an acrylic ruler with the first tick mark, with the long edge parallel to the sides of the block; align a horizontal line with the bottom of the block. Draw a line from the bottom of the square, through the tick mark, to the top of the square. **Repeat with each tick mark** until you have drawn all the vertical lines.

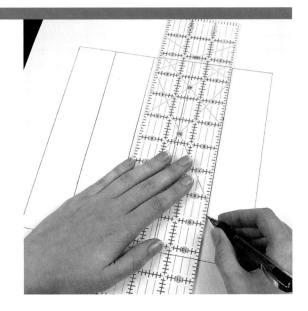

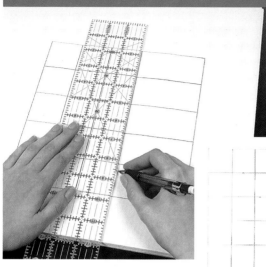

Rotate your block 90 degrees, so the bottom is now along a side. Repeat Steps 3 and 4, marking the increments with tick marks and then **drawing the remaining grid lines perpendicular to the first set, until the grid is complete.**

Tip

For a sampler quilt, make several copies of your grid to use for other blocks based on the same grid.

Working square by square, **draw each line of the original block onto the grid of the resized block, making sure the lines correspond exactly.** You may find it helpful to **color the pattern in as you go,** to keep track of where you are in the transferring process. Half-square triangles can be especially confusing, and coloring the pattern helps ensure that you draw the diagonal lines in the correct direction.

Making the Complex Simple

Let's say you want to draft a Storm at Sea block that finishes at 7 inches. While this pattern seems complex, drawing lines on top of the block to divide it into sections that can be easily pieced will result in an 8 × 8 grid. Use the flexible grid method to draft the unusual size for such a grid. Here are the answers to the questions on page 15: *finished block* = 7 inches; *divisions* = 8; *key number* = 8; *increment* = 1. Follow Steps 2 through 6 to resize the block. See page 107 for tips on making templates for piecing.

Tip

For a dramatic variation of Storm-at-Sea (see page 4), make partial blocks using the upper left 6 × 6 grid.

PIECED BLOCKS IN ANY SIZE

17

Stretching Blocks

I f you've been searching for the means to put a fresh face on your favorite traditional block, perhaps it's time to "give it a stretch." Even the most familiar traditional patterns assume an entirely new perspective when they are elongated into unexpected rectangular or diamond shapes. It may sound daunting, but take it from quilter and author Darra Duffy Williamson: If you can draw a square, you can draft these dynamic designs, too. In no time flat you'll have an inventive solution to your latest guild challenge or the beginning of a fabulous medallion quilt. So go ahead—stretch a block, and watch your creativity grow!

Getting Ready

What You'll Need

Metal ruler, 12" or longer

Sharp pencil or mechanical pencil

¼" graph paper

Colored pencils

Template material

Unlined paper

Protractor

Pair of frameless mirrors

Photocopier

You don't need anything unusual to draft the elongated blocks featured in this chapter: a pencil, ruler, and protractor will do the trick. Standard ¼-inch graph paper works just fine for drafting and designing with rectangles. You may find graph paper's squares distracting when working with the 60-degree diamond grids, though, so keep large (11 × 14-inch) unlined white paper or isometric (60-degree) graph paper on hand as well. Large pads of graph paper and isometric graph paper are available at many quilt shops and art or office supply centers. Oversize tracing or sketching paper, freezer paper, or plain newsprint are also options. Check your local quilt shop and "Resources" on page 126 for small, frameless mirrors; you can also have these cut at a glass-supply store.

Stretching Squares into Rectangles

Any grid-based block—a block that can be divided into an equal number of square units vertically and horizontally—can be stretched into a rectangle. Determine the number of grid squares in a single row of your block. Churn Dash has three squares across and down, so three is the key number. Your rectangle can measure any pair of numbers that are both multiples of three, such as 6 × 9 or 6 × 12 inches. Use a ruler and pencil to draw the desired rectangle on ¼-inch graph paper. Divide and mark each side of the rectangle into three equal segments. **"Connect the dots" to draw a grid.**

STRETCHING BLOCKS

Tip

Once you're comfortable with the process, try experimenting with grids divided into unequal segments.

2

Refer to your traditional square block. Begin with the square in the upper left-hand corner, and transfer the line from that square to the corresponding rectangle on your new grid. Continue square by square, row by row, **dividing each of the rectangular units horizontally, vertically, or diagonally, according to the original block drawing,** until you transfer the entire pattern onto the new grid. **Color as desired so you can clearly see the block pattern;** use the drawing to make templates, or rotary cut patches for piecing (see page 106).

Stretching Squares into Diamonds

1

When you stretch a block from a square into a diamond, not only the block but also every shape within the block becomes a diamond (or at least a portion of one). Since you will draft the block on a grid, you'll get the best results if you **select a block based on a 4-, 9-, or 16-patch grid, and one that includes more than one shape or shape sizes, such as one of the blocks shown.** Finally, choose a block without diagonal seams at the corners; you'll have fewer elongated points and seams to match when the finished blocks are joined.

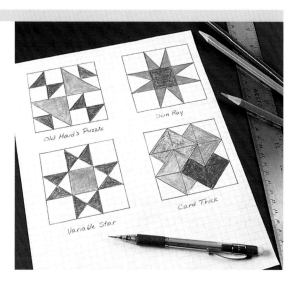

2

Keep the math simple. Choose a finished block size that can be divided evenly by the number of units in the block grid. For example, a Churn Dash block is based on a grid divided into three equal squares down by three across, so a finished block evenly divisible by three makes a good choice.

Use your ruler to draw a line parallel to and near the bottom corner of a large sheet of unlined paper. This line should measure the exact length of the finished size of the block (here, 9 inches). This line (AB) is your baseline.

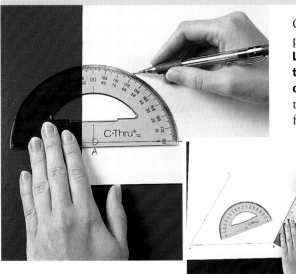

Carefully align the center baseline point of a protractor with Point A. **Locate the 60-degree mark on the protractor arc, and mark the paper with a dot at that point.** Remove the protractor and position your ruler carefully so it passes through both Point A and the dot. Draw a line equal in length to the baseline (in this case, 9 inches). Label the endpoint C.

Repeat, aligning the center baseline point of the protractor with Point B. **Draw a second 9-inch angled line parallel to AC.** Label the endpoint D.

Use your ruler to carefully connect the ends of the new angled lines, creating line CD. **The result is a perfect 60-degree diamond measuring 9 inches on each side.**

To create the Churn Dash block pattern, divide the diamond into an equal nine-patch grid, just as you would if you were working with a square. For a 9-inch block, measure along each side of the diamond and mark if off in 3-inch segments. **Connect the markings from side to opposite side to complete the diamond grid.**

Refer to your traditional square block. Beginning with the square in the upper left-hand corner, transfer the design from that square to the corresponding diamond in your newly drawn grid. **Divide each diamond unit horizontally, vertically, or diagonally, according to the original block drawing.** Work diamond by diamond, row by row, until you transfer the pattern of each square onto the corresponding diamond of the diamond-shaped grid. **Color your new block as desired.** Use this drawing to make templates for piecing; see page 107.

S T R E T C H I N G   B L O C K S

Working with Diamonds

Make reduced-size copies of your stretched block, and then use colored pencils to audition various color and value placements. A pair of frameless mirrors will help you preview the results possible when multiple stretched blocks are pieced and set together. **Align the mirrors on the sides of one obtuse (wide) angle of each diamond to see the results of combining three into a hexagon.** For a totally different look, **align the mirrors along one acute (narrow) angle, and you'll see how six diamonds can form a six-pointed star.**

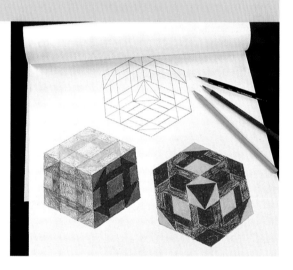

Dimensional Designs

By giving some thought to how you color or shade combinations of blocks, you can create all kinds of visual effects. For example, each block can be treated individually and colored in a low-contrast value range to get a dramatic, three-dimensional effect, like a large Tumbling Block. On the other hand, the same design can be colored from the center of the design outward, with little or no regard for block boundaries. The end result is a striking medallion-style design.

Tip

If your quilt center features a traditional square block, consider using a stretched version of that block for a striking border design.

Grain Considerations

Use your drawing to rotary cut or make templates for the patches in your block. (Remember to add seam allowances.) Be sure to keep the fabric grain in mind. You'll never have the straight grain on all outside edges of a diamond block because the angles aren't square. Either run the straight grain through the center of the block or take advantage of it on as many edges as possible. Just be consistent, and cut your patches consistently. **Mark the grain line arrows on your pattern and on each template, as a reminder.**

Bias Blues

Problem

When I try to assemble my diamond blocks, the patches stretch out of shape and the block ends up looking distorted.

Solution

Blocks made from diamonds have bias edges, both on the patches and the block perimeter. Tame those bias edges by using one or more of these methods.

❑ Before you press fabric that will be used for diamonds, give it an extra shot of spray starch. The stiffness of the fabric will help prevent the bias edges from stretching and fraying.

❑ Use freezer paper to make finished-size templates, and iron them onto your fabrics. When you join the patches, sew along the edge of the freezer paper, and the bias edges will be much less stretchy.

❑ For patches that have very sharp angles, trim off the tip of the sharp point about halfway between the point and the seam allowance. Your seam will be straighter without the point to skew out of alignment as you sew.

❑ Pin each seam extremely well. Match and pin seam intersections, the very ends of patches, and as many points between as you need to keep your edges aligned and your stitches straight for the entire length of the seam.

❑ Once your block is assembled, carefully stay-stitch ⅛ inch in from the edges. This will help keep the edges stabilized until they are sewn into the quilt top.

Press it right.

Pressing seam allowances along bias edges can be tricky. After you've taken pains to sew a straight seam, you don't want to stretch the patches out of shape with aggressive ironing. Instead, first set the seam: Press the seam as it was sewn without opening out either of the patches. Then unfold the patch you want to press the seam toward (usually the darker patch), and gently finger-press it into position. Set your hot, dry iron down on the seam without moving it from side to side or pushing the seam more fully open. If you don't get it right the first time, re-set the seam and try again.

Try This!

Stretch your block into a trapezoid.
A trapezoid is a square or rectangle with both sides angled in mirror image. Apply the same basic techniques of dividing up each side and drawing lines to correspond with those of the original block design. You'll create a sense of depth and perspective with blocks that seem to "loom" or recede into the distance. Turn every other block upside down to sew into rows.

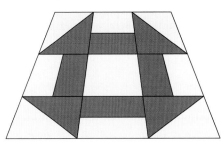

Wonderful
One Patch Quilts

Repetition of a single element throughout a quilt creates rhythm and unity in a design. Often the simplicity of such a plan leads to surprising strength and power. Our grandmothers knew that when they made charm quilts, in which they repeated the same shape throughout the quilt using a different fabric for each patch to keep the quilt interesting. Whether you follow that tradition or keep to a planned color palette, read on. Elsie Campbell shows you the variety of effects you can get from just one shape. Pick a shape, draft it to any size you want, and start playing!

Getting Ready

Look through books and visit quilt shows to see classic and contemporary One Patch quilts. Note how color is used in both antique and modern quilts to create interesting designs while using only a single template. While squares are the simplest One Patch pattern and the easiest to draft, you'd be amazed at the artful sophistication of many Amish One Patch quilts based on squares. Nine Patch quilts without alternate plain blocks may also be considered One Patch masterpieces. Triangles, rectangles, diamonds, pentagons, hexagons, octagons, and many other geometric shapes can create stunning designs. And the possibilities aren't limited to straight-sided shapes. Curved Clamshells and Apple Cores make for exciting One Patch quilts, though admittedly they're more of a challenge to piece.

Once you pick a shape to play with, fill a sheet of paper with the repeated design. Then photocopy it and use colored pencils to play with shading and color to create different designs. To make templates and piece your One Patch designs, see pages 107 and 111.

What You'll Need

- ¼" graph paper
- Isometric graph paper
- Plain paper
- Rulers
- Craft scissors
- Mechanical pencil
- Colored pencils
- Template plastic
- Compass

Exciting Possibilities from Simple Shapes

Rectangles: Bricks & Braids

A true rectangle is one that is exactly twice as long as it is tall. These proportions allow for some interesting arrangements. Placing the rectangles in **staggered rows yields a pattern known as Bricks,** which looks, of course, like a brick wall. **Positioning the rectangles in a perpendicular arrangement creates the Braids pattern.** Try setting this one on point and coloring the Braids so they look like a series of V shapes in vertical rows.

Half-Hexagons

1

Draft a hexagon, using isometric graph paper or using the instructions on page 77. **Then draw a line from the tip of one angle to the tip of the opposite one to divide the hexagon in half.** In order to explore the design possibilities on paper and also to cut patches from fabric, make a finished-size template. **Trace the drafted half-hexagon onto template plastic** and cut it out. Use the template as a guide for tracing repeats along the printed lines of isometric paper or on plain paper.

2

The geometry of the half-hexagon shape allows for many fun and easy patterns. Set end to end horizontally, they form orderly rows; for different effects, stagger the rows. To create the illusion of dimension, try the pattern called Inner City: Arrange the half-hexagons in pairs forming complete hexagons. **Draw groups of three hexagons, with the dividing lines all converging at the center of the group.** Place the light, medium, and dark colors in consistent positions to produce a 3-D look, as here and in the red quilt on page 24.

Equilateral Triangles

Rows of equilateral triangles form a Thousand Pyramids quilt. To draw an equilateral triangle (one with three 60-degree angles and sides of equal

The equilateral triangle can be divided to yield "kite" shapes, which are fun to play with in a One Patch design. Draw an equilateral triangle, then draw straight lines from the midpoint of each side to the opposite angle. **Outline one kite shape,** and make a finished-size template to trace around. Arrange your kites in rows by turning every other one upside down. Or place the narrow ends of six kites together to get a hexagon. Placing the wide ends together will take you back to an equilateral triangle. **Color your designs to audition various possibilities.**

Tip

Using the line that bisects the Kite, you can make a One Patch design like the blue quilt on page 24.

Darts: A Wide-Angle View

Another shape you can get from an equilateral triangle is known as the Dart. Draw lines from the midpoint of each side to the opposite angles. Then **outline one Dart,** and make a finished-size template to trace around. **Coloring the darts within a triangle with light, medium, and dark values** of the same color gives your triangle a three-dimensional look, like a pyramid seen from above. Or you can simply arrange them in rows, turning every other one upside down.

Apple Core

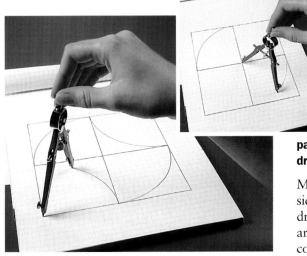

To draft the classic Apple Core, draw a square with sides equal to the desired length of your patch. Divide the square in half vertically and horizontally, creating four quadrants. Set your compass to span one quadrant. **Position the point of the compass in the center of the square and draw arcs in two opposite quadrants.**

Move the compass point to the outside corner of an empty quadrant and draw an arc, connecting the first two arcs. **Repeat in the fourth quadrant** to complete the Apple Core.

Make a finished-size template for tracing from your drawing, and use it to **trace rows of nested Apple Core patches, turning every other one sideways.** Make reduced copies of your drawing and play with different color schemes and color placements to find a design you like. Remember to add seam allowances when cutting fabric patches! See the opposite page for tips on piecing these designs.

Clamshell

Another fun curved design is the Clamshell. Draw a square with sides that are equal to the desired height and width of your Clamshell. Set your compass to span half a side of the square. **Position the point of the compass at the exact center of the square and draw an arc in the upper half of the square.** Move the point of the compass to the lower left corner and draw an arc from side to side. **Repeat in the lower right corner** to complete your design.

Tip

Insert an occasional patch in an accent color to bring visual excitement to your quilt.

Use this clamshell drawing to make a finished-size template for tracing. **Trace the template to make rows of nested Clamshells.** Photocopy the drawing, reducing it to a convenient scale, and use these copies to play with color combinations and value placements. Add seam allowances when cutting your patches from fabric. See the opposite page for tips on piecing these curved designs.

The Quilter's Problem Solver

Taking the Fear Out of Piecing Curves

Problem

I'd love to make an Apple Core or Clamshell quilt, but I have trouble getting patches like these to fit together and lie flat when sewn.

Solution

Follow these simple steps to hand-sew perfect curved seams every time. (If you prefer to piece curves by machine, see page 110.)

1. Cut out a freezer paper template for each shape in your quilt. Use a hot, dry iron to press each template, shiny side down, onto the wrong side of your chosen fabric.

2. Cut out each patch a scant ¼ inch beyond the freezer paper template. Clip into the seam allowances along sharp curves to ensure that your piece will lie flat. Use the tip of the iron to press the seam allowances to the wrong side of each patch.

3. Position your patches on a design wall and examine your arrangement for easiest assembly. Some patterns fall into horizontal or vertical rows, like the blue quilt on page 24. Others assemble more easily diagonally, like the purple Clamshells on the same page.

4. Remove the patches two at a time, and place adjacent edges together with right sides facing. Use a thread in a color that will match or blend, and blindstitch the edges together with small, closely spaced stitches.

5. Continue adding patches, removing the freezer paper from a patch only after it has been completely surrounded by other patches.

Skill Builder

Set in seams with ease.

Many patterns, including One Patch patterns, have angled seams between rows. To sew the rows together, you must set patches into these angled seams. For the best results, keep these tips in mind.

❏ Keep the seam allowances unsewn at the edges and corners of patches. It's best to mark the intersection of the ¼-inch seam allowances on the wrong side of each patch so you can see them when you're sewing.

❏ Backstitch at the beginning and end of every seam. This will ensure that your angled seams won't have gaping holes.

❏ Sew each side of a set-in patch with a separate seam. Resist the urge to pivot and continue along an adjacent seam; this can produce puckers and creases in your finished product.

Try This!

Choose a happy ending.

Unless your One Patch shape is a square or rectangle, the outside edges of your quilt top will be irregular. Try one of these finishing methods.

❏ Sew borders all around, stitching through the One Patches. Cut away the parts of the One Patches that extend beyond the seam allowances.

❏ Appliqué the quilt center to your border strips.

❏ Create a knife-edge finish: Turn the quilt top and backing edges ¼ inch to the inside (covering the edges of the batting), and blindstitch the folded edges together.

❏ Bind the shaped edges, using bias binding to ease around curves and mitering at every angle.

Appliquéing
the Big Picture

I f you're a fan of those gorgeous pictorial wall quilts, you're in luck. Now you, too, can create an original work of quilt art, starting with a photograph or picture. See your favorite flower, still-life scene, animal, or any image at all enlarged to a size that will really command attention. Read on as quilt artist Charlotte Warr Andersen shares her secrets for enlarging any photo or design to create a spectacular appliqué masterpiece.

Getting Ready

Find a photo that you want to turn into an appliqué quilt. Photos that translate into a good quilt are usually simple, with an interesting composition of elements. Also, consider the subject matter—if it's exciting to you, you're more likely to translate it well into fabric. Flowers and plants lend themselves especially well to this technique because you can depart from the original photo considerably and still produce a fabric image that's recognizable. Look for large, plain paper, such as no-seam paper or Alpha Numeric paper at drafting or art supply stores, or tape together smaller sheets until you have one sheet large enough to make a full-size pattern.

In this chapter are three ways to enlarge a photo: using a grid, a photocopier, or various projectors. Choose one method to complete your actual-size pattern. Then refer to page 112 for tips on using the appliqué technique of your choice to translate your design to fabric.

What You'll Need

Photo or picture

Calculator

Write-on transparency film (available at office supply stores)

Fine-point, permanent markers

Clear acrylic rulers

Freezer paper or other paper large enough for a full-size pattern

Pencil

Clear or masking tape

Optional:

   Photocopier

   Overhead projector

   Slide projector

   Opaque projector

Grid Enlargements

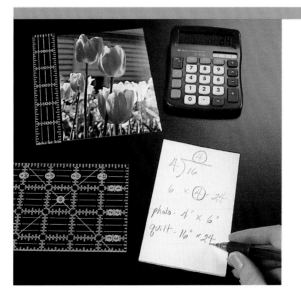

The basic method for enlarging a photo or picture, and one you can do with simple tools, is the paper-and-pencil, one-to-one grid. First, decide how large you want the quilt design to be. As an example, let's say you want to translate a 4 × 6 photo into a quilt that will be 16 inches wide. Divide the width of the photo (4) into the desired width (16) to determine your enlargement factor (we'll call it the EF)—in this case, 4. **Multiply the length of your picture, in this case 6 inches, by the EF, and the enlarged wallhanging will be 16 × 24 inches.**

2

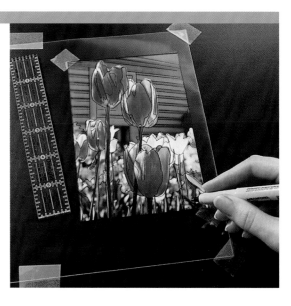

Place a sheet of write-on transparency film on top of the photo, and tape both in place so they don't shift. **Using a fine-point, permanent black marker, trace the main features in the photo onto the film.** As you trace the shapes, try to picture them being four times their size (or whatever your quilt's EF is), and leave out any shapes that will be too small to appliqué even when they are enlarged. Any shapes that look too complicated after enlarging can be changed or cleaned up when you finalize your enlarged pattern.

3

Using a different color permanent marker and a clear acrylic ruler, **draw a ½-inch grid (horizontal and vertical lines spaced ½ inch apart) on your photo overlay.** On paper large enough for a full-size pattern, **draw a grid with the same number of squares as on your photo, but in a size multiplied by the EF.** In this example, there are 12 rows of 8 squares each; the large sheet will have the same arrangement, but each square will be four times the size (4 × ½ = 2), or 2 inches square.

4

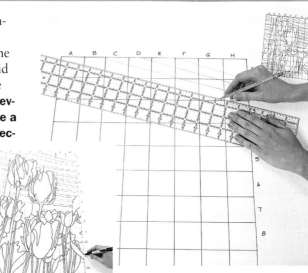

Label the grid with letters and numbers on the top and side (as on a map) for easy reference. Transfer the lines in each square of the small grid to the corresponding squares in the larger grid. **Continue lines across several squares as appropriate, and use a ruler to draw straight lines where necessary.** After the entire design has been transferred in this way, **go over your lines in permanent marker for a finished, enlarged drawing.** This will serve as the master pattern for your appliqué.

Photocopier Enlargements

To enlarge your design on a copy machine, make an overlay and trace the photo as described in Step 2 on the opposite page. Take the overlay to a copy center. Some have copiers that can make copies up to 36 × 48 inches for just a few dollars. If neccessary, enlarge your design in sections, then tape them together.

Use an enlargement factor (see page 31), **a proportional scale (see page 13) or a photocopying percentage chart (see page 118) to determine how much to enlarge your image.**

Check the yellow pages directory for drafting or blueprint stores. These stores can make extra-large copies.

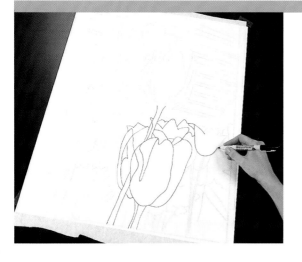

Once you have made a photocopied enlargement, make a clean copy of the pattern by hand. The width of the original lines is now enlarged at the same percentage as the entire image, and the lines are undoubtedly fuzzy. Place a clean sheet of paper on top of the enlarged copy. Use freezer paper if you prefer, and tape together sheets if necessary. **Trace all the lines with a fine-point permanent marker.** You'll get the best results by tracing in the center of the thick, enlarged lines.

Make sure that all shapes are fully enclosed by lines so you'll know how to cut out each appliqué piece.

Projections

A Clear Image on Your Wall

Projecting the actual picture that you want to enlarge will help you produce a design much closer to the original. You can assess various sizes of projections to determine just how big you want the quilt to be, and you can decide more easily which details to include and which to modify.

Cut a sheet of paper (or tape pieces together) until you have a piece at least as big as the desired finished size of your quilt. Tape it to the wall. Project the image onto the paper, and move the projector until the image is the size you want. **Trace the design lines.**

Be cautious when using projection to enlarge a design with long, straight lines, as part of the design will be distorted.

APPLIQUÉING THE BIG PICTURE

Slide Projector

Slides usually give a clear, sharp picture with good detail. Either take pictures on slide film, or have a local camera store make a slide from your image for a few dollars. If you don't own a slide projector, ask around: chances are a friend, co-worker, or family member does. Pop the slide into the slide projector, then set it up to project the image on the wall. Tape paper onto the wall, turn off the lights, position the projector so the image is the size you want, and trace the image onto the paper.

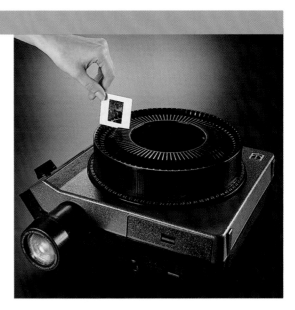

Opaque Projector

With an opaque projector, you do not need to have a slide. Tape paper onto a wall and **place the photo under the projector.** Position the projector until your image on the paper is the size you want it, and trace it. For the clearest image, you'll need to use an opaque projector in the dark, so draw the shades or wait until nighttime.

Overhead Projector

Overhead projectors are commonly found in schools, so if you know a teacher, ask to borrow the school equipment or use it in the classroom after school is out for the day. To begin, you'll need to have a transparency made of your picture. Copy stores can transfer your photo onto transparency film very easily and inexpensively, or if you have a scanner and printer, you may be able to make your own transparency. Once you have your transparency, tape your paper on a wall, **place the transparency on the bed of the projector,** project the image onto the paper, and trace.

Designing from Your Enlargement

1

Choose fabrics to reflect the colors and textures of the object you are portraying. Don't feel you have to stick to fabrics that look exactly like the photo. Spice up a somber design with plaid, polka dot, or print fabrics that contain the colors or moods you want to convey. To provide a sense of depth and liveliness in your quilt, choose fabrics with good contrast for dark and light areas.

2

To transfer shapes from your paper pattern to fabric, place your pattern on a lighted surface. Position the fabric right side up on top of the appropriate portion of the pattern, so that the fabric design complements the shape. For example, place curved striations in a mottled fabric so they follow the contours of a petal, **then draw the shape of the appliqué onto the fabric using your preferred fabric marker.** You may find this easier if you tape your drawing and the fabric in place, especially when drawing curves.

Tip

You don't need to go out and buy a light box. A large, sunny window makes a great substitute.

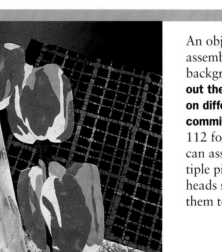

3

An object such as a flower can be assembled independently from the background. This way, you can **try out the main elements of your design on different backgrounds before you commit to one fabric.** Refer to page 112 for unit appliqué techniques. You can assemble the elements of a multiple piece appliqué such as the tulip heads shown here, and then appliqué them to a background.

Tip

When you're auditioning background fabrics, you can stay true to the original image or try something completely different.

APPLIQUÉING THE BIG PICTURE

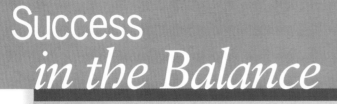

W e've all wondered from time to time what to do to make a quilt more dynamic. That's when we could benefit from a greater understanding of basic design principles such as balance, symmetry, and proportion. While these may seem like dry, academic terms, putting the concepts into practice will contribute to your quilt's visual impact and power to captivate. By manipulating shapes and elements, you'll create harmony, unity, and excitement in your quilts. And while you're learning the basics of good design from quilt artist Karen Eckmeier, you'll have fun, too!

Getting Ready

Effective use of some basic design principles will help you create a quilt that looks more interesting. Whether you tend toward a planned, traditional design or a more random or modern one, the design principles described here will help your quilt hold the viewer's attention. Take time to play. Try out some of the visual exercises from this chapter, concentrating on just one block or on a whole quilt design. Don't settle on a plan until you've rearranged and played with the various elements of your design in several different ways.

You may wish to start with a simple, asymmetrical shape, as we have in the steps that follow. Layer construction paper and cut out multiples of your shape. Also enlarge and reduce the shape on a photocopier, and cut out several repeats. If you like to appliqué, play with curved shapes; if piecing is your preference, experiment with a simple triangle or diamond.

What You'll Need

- **Construction paper**
- **Scissors**
- **Fabrics**
- **Pencil**
- **Eraser**
- **Pair of frameless mirrors**
- **Photocopier**

Design Principles

Mood & Motion

Depending on the mood you want to create in your design, choose and place the elements and motifs to show either exciting movement or calm restfulness. **The shapes you choose to work with play a large part.** Man-made geometric shapes, such as squares and other wide-angled polygons, are formal, flat, and static. They rest in the design without creating motion. Triangles and other shapes with narrow angles actually point the eye in a direction and give the illusion of movement. Circles and similar shapes that include curves create a sense of spinning and motion.

Symmetry

Balance in a design means that both sides are similar in terms of content—your eye sees an equivalent amount of elements dispersed all around. Symmetry, or perfect balance, results when identical elements occur on both sides of the design or at the top and bottom of a design. **You can hold a mirror next to a design or motif** to see how it looks when it is part of a symmetrical design. **Use symmetry when you want perfect balance, which results in a more traditional, formal design.**

Double Symmetry

Double symmetry means that the design suggests a mirror image from side to side and from top to bottom. **Hold two mirrors at a 90-degree angle near a motif to audition it for double symmetry.** Or divide your design area into four quadrants, and repeat the mirror image of the same motif or elements in each quadrant for an impeccably balanced design. **Designs with double symmetry also tend to be fairly formal.**

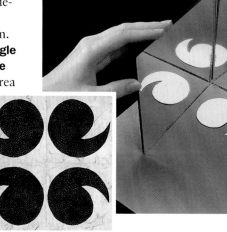

Radial Symmetry

In radial symmetry, the design is balanced around a center point, and the visual weight is distributed evenly from the center outward. These designs are usually circular, as in a Dresden Plate, Mariner's Compass, or floral wreath. **A spiral or circular design can create a sense of spinning, rotating motion.** To quickly see a radial design, **tape two mirrors together at a narrow angle, then place them next to your motif or a section of your block.**

Asymmetry

In an asymmetrically balanced design, shapes and lines are distributed evenly, but they are not arranged as mirror images. Pictorial blocks and quilts are often asymmetrical. Balance is achieved in asymmetry through repetition of the design elements and approximately equal "weight" (distribution of the motifs) on all sides of a design. This informal type of balance can create energy and excitement.

Proportion

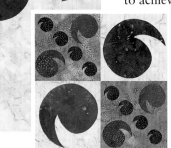

Proportion is the relationship of the sizes of your design elements. **For good design, consider grouping several smaller elements to balance single, larger elements.** A simple way to achieve this is to work in multiples of a basic measurement: In a 6-inch block, for example, use two motifs that are 3 inches in size, four 1½-inch motifs, and eight ¾-inch motifs. **Space them throughout the design using symmetry** or asymmetry.

Create visual energy by using odd numbers of motifs in your designs or odd numbers of blocks in a quilt.

Position

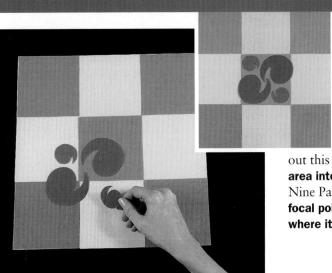

Quilts with the main attraction placed at the center tend to have a formal look. On the other hand, when the focal point is off-center, the design may be more interesting, whimsical, organic, or fresh. To try out this concept, **divide your design area into a tic-tac-toe grid** (like a Nine Patch block) **and place your focal point at one of the intersections, where it will be just off center.**

For greater emphasis, contrast white or light background areas near the focal point with darker colors surrounding it.

Repetition

A repeating or rhythmic design does not have a single focal point but suggests gentle motion through the use of equally spaced elements or motifs. These designs tend to have equal emphasis on shape and line over the entire composition. Be sure to leave a little "breathing space." Motifs that occupy all the visual space of a quilt are powerful, but they can be overwhelming. **Regular spacing that alternates with plainer areas** (as in a checkerboard) gives the eye a chance to rest and creates a more pleasing composition.

Unity

Repeating an element or motif throughout a quilt can also help to unify a design. This small quilt includes many different colors, patterns, and fabrics, but repeating the comma motif throughout the quilt in appliqués and quilting designs ties together what would otherwise be very disparate elements.

Straight-Line Directionality

Tip

Use sashing strips or bars of contrasting fabric to inject directionality for the look and mood you want.

A design with horizontal layers is calming, drawing your eyes slowly from side to side. **If, however, the dominant elements in your design run vertically, the effect tends to be higher energy** and more visual excitement. As you sketch a design or arrange motifs or blocks on a design wall, try out schemes with the "layers" running horizontally, then vertically.

Diagonals

A strong diagonal element in your design causes the viewer's eye to sweep from one corner to the opposite one and back again, giving your design a sense of movement. A line can be a specific, linear element or **it can be implied by the arrangement of a group of motifs** or design elements in a row. **The placement of fabrics and colors within a block such as a Jacob's Ladder** or Irish Chain creates diagonal movement as well.

Tip

A diagonal arrangement allows you to play with balance. Try using two contrasting colors or one "full" side and one "empty" one.

S or Z

Diagonal S- or Z-shape designs create a path for the eye to follow and therefore they create a sense of movement that may be either flowing and relaxing or jerky and electrifying. **You can experiment with this composition by playing with lines on paper.** As with a diagonal, **try using two contrasting colors on either side of your line.** Or keep to one color, but use darks and lights opposite one another.

Visual Weight

When you're creating a design, whether it's a realistic landscape or an abstract design, **keep the visual weight toward the bottom,** as in nature. We're used to seeing heavier, darker objects (trees, rocks, and land) in the lower portion of our vision and lighter objects (sky and clouds) toward the top. Designs with the visual weight at the top leave us unsettled; it's unnatural for us to see things in the world around us this way because they seem to be upside down.

Tip

In a traditional patchwork quilt, too, place more of the visually weighty pieces—larger patches and darker colors— toward the bottom.

SUCCESS IN THE BALANCE

Design Your
Own Block

You've gone the safe route, following patterns or books to make your quilts. Now take the next step with quilt designer Karen Eckmeier. Cultivate your sense of adventure and nurture your creativity by designing an original quilt block. Fans of patchwork may want to start out with a favorite traditional block and add, subtract, or skew lines to create a unique, new look. Or use a pictorial image as the basis for something unique, either pieced or appliquéd. After a few simple exercises, you'll find out what a kick it is to design your own pattern, and your quiltmaking will never be the same!

Getting Ready

First, do some research. Gather up books of classic blocks and bookmark some of your favorites to use as starting points. You'll probably get the most creative fun from blocks that are not too complex. Three or four divisions within a block will provide plenty of possibilities. If appliqué is your technique of choice, gather photos, simple sketches, children's coloring books, art books, and postcards from art museums. Leaf through them to find images that appeal to you.

Second, get ready to experiment. Free your mind of any restrictions on how things are supposed to look.

Get out graph paper, tracing paper, and pencils, both lead and colored. Of course, if you're an adventurous techie, you can use a software program and the exact same principles explained in this chapter to design your own block on the computer. (See page 48 for more information.)

(See page 48 for more information.)

What You'll Need

- **Graph paper**
- **Pencil**
- **Tracing paper**
- **Ruler**
- **A book of quilt block patterns**
- **Optional:**
  - **Compass**
  - **Light box**

Manipulating Traditional Patchwork Blocks

Using Part of a Block

Orange Peel block

Look closely at one of your favorite blocks, and isolate a portion that looks like it would be interesting or fun to work with. The traditional Orange Peel pattern, for example, offers lots of possibilities for experimentation. **Try manipulating just one section or unit of the block into alternating positions, mirror images, and varied sizes for new and different combinations.**

Draft your own Orange Peel pattern following the directions on page 70.

Draft your own Orange Peel pattern following the directions on page 70.

DESIGN YOUR OWN BLOCK

Add Lines

Start with a drafting of your classic block or a part of the block, such as this section of the Orange Peel. **Add a line, dividing a large area into smaller ones.** You can make your design variation symmetrical by adding the same line in all identical areas, or concentrate on just one area. Then draw your new block and **try out different arrangements of groups of four** to see if interesting secondary patterns emerge from the combinations.

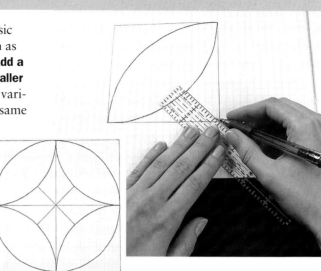

Delete Lines

Deleting lines from a block can also yield fun and interesting new variations.
It can also give you that extra-large space you need to show off a favorite print fabric or a theme print.
Again, **try out different arrangements and combinations of your block to see what designs form.**

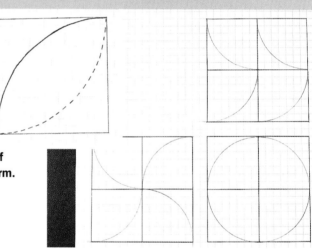

Changing the Grid

Another way to use traditional blocks as springboards for new designs is to alter the basic grid of your chosen block. Instead of drawing your block on an even, square grid, **draw a rectangular or diamond-shaped grid,** then fill in the resulting patches to create the new block.

Step off the straight and narrow path with curved grid lines instead of straight ones. Keep the outer edges of the block the same, and stick to the same basic grid dimensions. **However, replace your grid lines with free-form curves.** Your design will have a new sense of whimsy, but it will still be recognizable as a version of the original block. Once you get going with these variations, you'll be amazed at the new creations you can invent.

Tip

If you're not comfortable drawing curves freehand, use a flexible curve (see page 88).

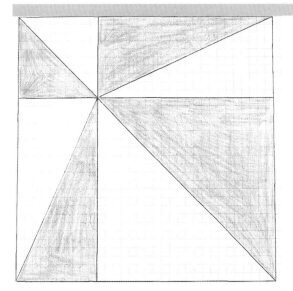

Shifting the grid is a great way to give a traditional block a new look. **Instead of drawing the grid for this pinwheel with four equal squares, the lines were shifted and just two of the four patches are the same size.** To take it a step further, graduate the size of your patches from one corner to another. Combine these kinds of blocks in mirror image for some mind-boggling effects.

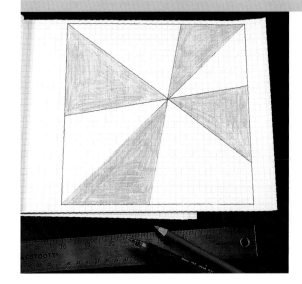

Another fun variation is to **draw your grid lines at an angle to the block outline.** Divide these nonsquare sections just as you would square ones and take a look at the new spin on your traditional block. If it's a little too much, try keeping one set of grid lines (either horizontal or vertical) parallel to the block outline, and slanting only the ones in the other direction.

DESIGN YOUR OWN BLOCK

5

Another fun way to alter your favorite block is to **substitute curved lines for the straight ones that form the outer edges of the block.** Draw the block on graph paper, then tape tracing paper over it. On the tracing paper, draw gently curved lines in place of the straight outer lines. Use a compass to impose perfect arcs on your design, or draw the curves freehand. Refer to the photo on page 42 for an example of this technique using the Orange Peel block.

Tip

Tip

Appliqué curved blocks onto a background or sashing strips, and you won't have to worry about complex piecing.

Creating from Nature

1

You can use a real-life item from nature to make your own patchwork pattern. Place the item on a light box, and tape a piece of graph paper over it. **Trace the outline as well as you can, altering the shape slightly as needed to follow the printed lines on the graph paper.** Where necessary, draw diagonal lines across the graph paper squares to simulate curved portions.

2

Once you trace the entire image, **work on the graph paper outline to straighten curves, simplify lines, and extend lines from angles.** Consider various strategies for piecing the block or portions of the block. If you must set in angles along the edges, see page 111 for instructions. To give your image visual depth, imagine a source of light, and **shade areas closest to the light in pale tones and areas furthest from the light or in the shadows in darker tones.** Scout for fabrics close to your chosen shadings.

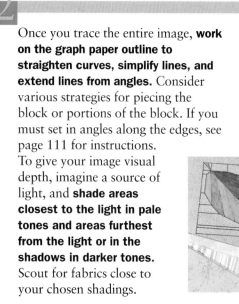

Isolating Designs

Sometimes it's hard to appreciate a single flower in the midst of a large garden. Similarly, there can be a great block design hiding within almost any large, pictorial image. To find these hidden treasures, make a viewing window. **Cut a 2-inch-square opening in a piece of lightweight cardboard and move it around on any image**—a picture in a book, a photograph, even a piece of large-print fabric. Focus on the lines and shapes, not the actual image.

Tip

Tape a piece of colored cellophane inside your window to mute the colors and allow you to focus solely on the shapes.

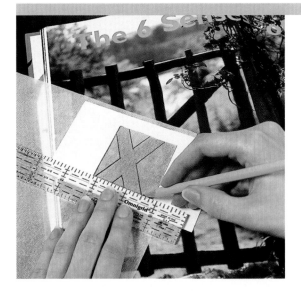

When you find an area that you like, **place a piece of tracing paper over it and transfer the lines and shapes.** Repeat to make a total of 16 tracings, and cut them out so you can play with different arrangements of your newly created block.

As you play with your tracings, vary their positions and orientations within an arrangement. **A set of four blocks may indicate the potential of your block.** Watch for secondary designs, continuing lines, and groups of shapes that create motion and excitement in your new design. Keep in mind the basic design principles of balance and repetition (see page 36) as you repeat and rotate your image.

Tip

Turn some of the tracings to the reverse side to explore mirror images of your design. Darken or retrace the lines for better visibility.

DESIGN YOUR OWN BLOCK

Creating on
the Computer

There are so many quilt-design software programs out there, how's a quilter to know which one is best? Let author and award-winning quiltmaker Gloria Hansen introduce you to some of her favorites—from basic block libraries to programs that enable you to produce sophisticated designs of your own invention. No matter what your skill level on the computer or in quilting, you'll be able to draft beautiful quilts at warp speed. Your computer will also become a very handy tool for auditioning different settings, calculating yardages, and providing rotary cutting directions, actual-size templates, and even foundations.

Getting Ready

To choose a software program, first decide what you want your software to do for you. Do you have a block in mind for a quilt and want to see how it would look in different settings? Maybe you just want quick foundations printed for a favorite block. Have an idea for an original pieced or appliquéd block and need help getting the dimensions just right? Perhaps you want to manipulate blocks to create a new design altogether. All of these options are demonstrated on the next several pages so you can get a feel for what some of the programs can do. But that's just the tip of the iceberg: With thousands of quilt blocks, dozens of design tools, and enough options to produce nearly any block under the sun, you're sure to be wowed by how computers can help you with the drafting and design of anything from a simple motif to a complex king-size quilt layout.

First, take a look at the "demos" in this chapter. Then, refer to "Which Software Is Right for Me?" on page 56 to determine what software program best suits your needs. Also check "Resources" on page 126 for related Web sites that you can visit for tips, tutorials, and helpful links.

While much of the quilt software is made for PCs only, Mac users with a recent model Macintosh are not abandoned. A software program called Virtual PC (see "Resources" on page 126) installs a full PC operating system on your Mac. When you launch Virtual PC, you have the Windows operating system sitting in the middle of your Macintosh operating system, allowing you to have the best of both worlds. In any case, be sure to check the system requirements carefully before purchasing any software.

Block Software

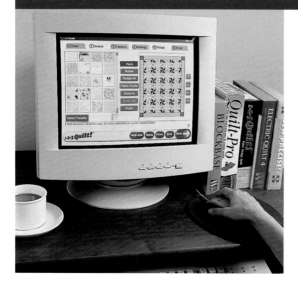

1

There are many quilting software programs, and you may want to invest in more than one. Computer and/or quilt design novices may do best to start with a software program that provides blocks. These run the gamut, from predrawn blocks that you can arrange into canned quilt layouts, to programs that let you recolor and lay out blocks in a variety of sets, to software that helps you draw and manipulate your own designs. Some programs even include scanned fabric "swatches" that you can insert into your design.

2

There are many software packages tha contain quilt blocks. We've picked the most extensive one to show you: **Blockbase** is the CD-ROM version of Barbara Brackman's *Encyclopedia of Pieced Quilt Patterns*. It includes over 4,000 quilt blocks—every pattern published from 1835 to 1970. **Search tools help you find the block you want,** or you can browse through all the blocks, then select the one you want to work with by simply clicking the mouse.

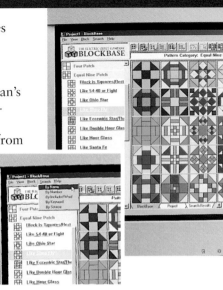

3

Blockbase gives you several print options for your block. **From the File menu, choose Print,** then click on the information you want printed out. You can choose the size of your block, the width of the seam allowances, and the thickness of your lines. **The printout will include all the information you need for your preferred cutting and piecing method:** A labeled reference block, complete templates for the block, and the number of patches needed (with rotary cutting instructions).

Sew Precise!

Sew Precise! is a foundation block program; all the blocks in this collection can be sewn using foundations. **Choose the block you want to make,** then use the print menu to **specify the size of your block and the format of your foundation printout.** You can also specify the width of your seam allowances before you print out the foundations. While standard printer paper will work, special papers are available for printing foundation patterns.

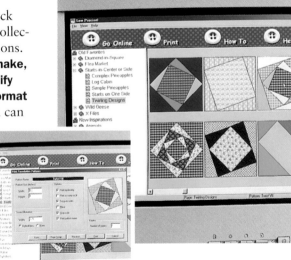

Tip

Products such as Crystal Paper (see "Resources" on page 126) feed through the printer smoothly and tear away easily.

Quilt Design for Novices: 1-2-3 Quilt!

1

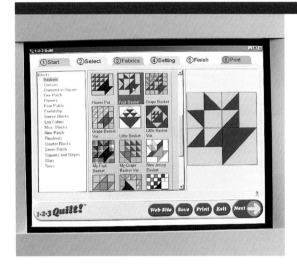

1-2-3 Quilt! is an easy program for those new to computer designing. Its step-by-step approach walks you through designing a basic quilt using any of the traditional pieced blocks included with the program. It has a friendly approach that gives even the novice computer user the confidence to design a basic quilt. **Begin at the Select tab and choose one of the 500 blocks to use in your quilt.**

2

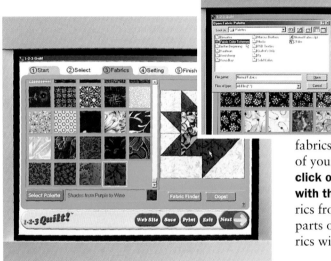

To color your block, proceed to the Fabrics tab. Click on the Select Palette button to **see the list of fabric collections available to you for designing your block.** Double-click on fabric collections until your fabrics appear as swatches to the left of your block. **Click on a fabric, then click on a patch in the block to fill it with that fabric.** You can select fabrics from different palettes for various parts of your block and replace fabrics with a click of the mouse.

Tip

Make coloring easy with three clicks of your mouse. Click on the Fabric Finder button, a fabric in the block, and then the patch you want to fill.

3

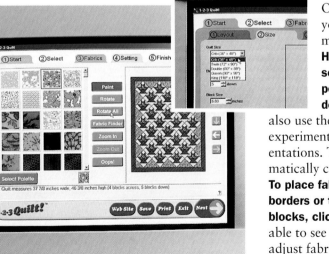

Once you're happy with your block, you're ready to move to the Setting tab. **Here, you'll decide on the setting (straight or on-point), size, sashing, borders, and binding.** You can also use the "Rotate" button to experiment with different block orientations. The program will automatically create your quilt layout. **To place fabrics in the sashing and borders or to adjust fabrics in the blocks, click the Finish tab.** You'll be able to see the entire quilt layout and adjust fabrics accordingly.

CREATING ON THE COMPUTER

4

You can keep going "back to the drawing board," adjusting the size of the block, the setting, or any other aspect of the quilt as you design. **Once you're satisfied with your quilt design, it's time to print.** The Print tab lets you print quilt information, including the block, the quilt, a rotary cutting chart, a yardage chart, and templates. Choose the information you want to print out by clicking on the appropriate boxes.

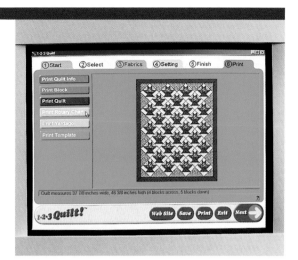

Altering and Designing Blocks: Quilt-Pro

1

Some quilt design programs include both quilt blocks and drawing tools. When designing an original block on the computer, it's often easier to manipulate an existing block. These steps describe how to do this using Quilt-Pro, but the method is similar for other quilt programs.

First, select a block. The block will open onto a work area, a large space similar to a gridded design wall. By using your program's toolbar, you can manipulate your block into a design you like.

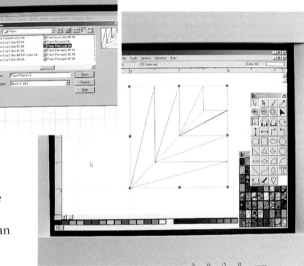

2

Before working with a block, "group" it so all of its patches will act as a unit. Then, as you stretch, resize, or rotate the block, each patch will follow along. Select the whole block with the "Select" tool (the solid arrow): **Click, hold, and drag to include the whole block inside the resulting box.** Release the mouse, and square handles will appear, indicating that the block is selected. **Go to the Effects menu, then select Group.** If you want to ungroup them later so you can manipulate patches individually, choose Ungroup from the Effects drop-down menu.

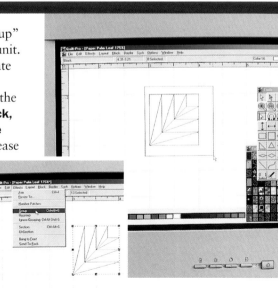

CREATING ON THE COMPUTER

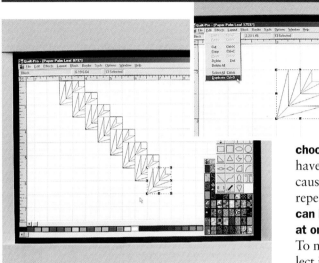

Before you start manipulating your block, duplicate it so you won't have to reload it time and time again. To make copies, make sure the block is selected (it will show those square handles at the sides). **Go to the Edit menu and choose Duplicate.** Repeat until you have as many copies as you want. Because your design surface is large and repeats can overlap each other, **you can have a large number of copies all at once without running out of room.** To move a block, click and hold to select it, then drag it to a new position.

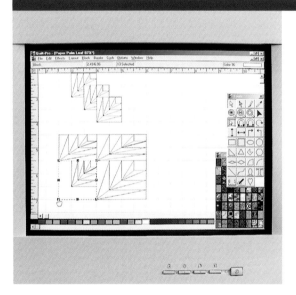

To resize or reshape the block, click on it once to select it. Place your cursor on one of the handles, then click, hold, and drag the block into its new size or shape. **Try out many different block manipulations, then try them together in different arrangements.** The rulers and the grid will help you keep track of the sizes of your "new" blocks.

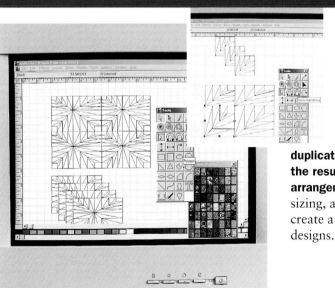

The arrows on the toolbar are for rotating patches, blocks, or grouped blocks. Once you create an arrangement of modified blocks that you like and want to work with, group them (see Step 2 on the opposite page). **Then duplicate your new group, and rotate the resulting groupings into various arrangements.** By duplicating, re-sizing, and rotating blocks, you can create a wealth of exciting new designs.

Tip

To keep your blocks in line, select Grid Snap from the Options menu and their corners will always be at a corner of your grid.

Tip

Pulling a corner handle increases or decreases the block's height and width together. The handles on the sides change only one dimension at a time.

Tip

If you want a larger selection of fabrics, visit the Quilt-Pro Web site at www. quiltpro.com and download the latest fabric design scans for free.

CREATING ON THE COMPUTER

Creating an Original Appliqué Design

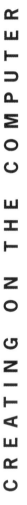

1

Many quilt design programs include tools for drawing appliqué designs. Some even have predrawn shapes that you can customize—meaning you don't have to have drawing skills to create lovely appliqué patterns. Here's an overview of this technique using Electric Quilt 4 (EQ4); other design programs work in a similar manner.

Select Work on Block from the Worktable drop-down menu. Then go to the Block menu and select New Block, then Patchdraw. The Patch-draw toolbar will appear on your work area.

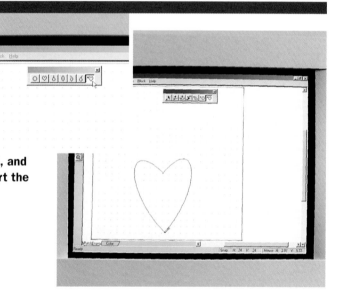

2

On the toolbar, click on the shape you wish to draw in the drawing area. To draw a heart, for example, **click on the heart on the toolbar to select it,** then move your cursor to the drawing area, where the cursor will change into a pencil. **Click, hold, and drag the mouse to create a heart the size you want.**

3

Tip

If you want to select multiple shapes, hold down the "Shift" key as you click.

To edit, move, or manipulate a shape, click on the "Select" tool (the solid arrow on the toolbar). When you click on the shape, **handles (small square boxes) appear around the shape,** indicating that it is selected. It may take some practice to select your shape—you need to click exactly on part of the line of your heart for the handles to show.

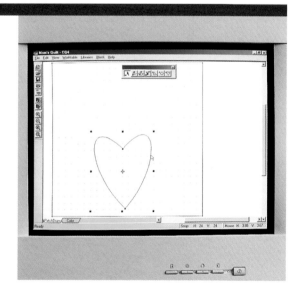

4

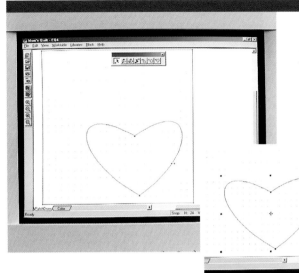

Use your mouse to click, hold, and drag one of the handles to change the shape of your heart. Note that the handles disappear momentarily as you reshape the heart; **as soon as you release the mouse button, they reappear.**

Tip

To move a shape within the drawing area, click and hold anywhere inside it, then drag it to the new location.

5

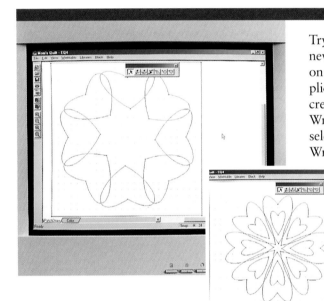

Try playing with multiples of your new shape. Use the Symmetry feature on the Block drop-down menu to duplicate, flip, or rotate it. Go on to create a circular repeat with the Wreathmaker feature. For example, select your heart shape, choose Wreathmaker, then experiment with cluster settings **until you get a nicely spaced combination of hearts in the round.**

For a more complex repeat design, draw two nested hearts, then select both shapes and use the Wreathmaker—**your new design will include both hearts.**

6

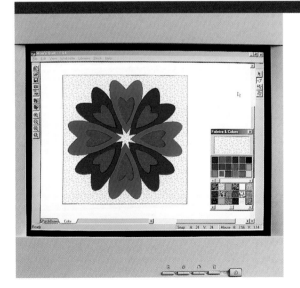

To color in your design, click the Color tab at the bottom of your screen. A color palette will appear next to your worktable. **Click on a color or fabric from the palette, then click inside the shape or shapes you want to fill.** If you like to use color to help you design, you can switch back and forth between the Patchdraw area and the Color area to add or remove shapes and change or add color as you go.

Tip

To correct any "oops," select Undo from the Edit drop-down menu.

CREATING ON THE COMPUTER

55

Which Software Is Right for Me?

This chapter has barely scratched the surface of what design programs can do. To help you decide which program is best for you, this handy chart calls out some of the more important features of several products on the market. Nothing, though, can replace a hands-on tryout. To make a better-informed decision, visit a friend, quilt shop, or quilt show where you can see and use the software. Most of these programs require a PC with a minimum operating system of Windows 95 or 98, plus a CD-ROM. Mac users can purchase Virtual PC and run almost any program PC users can. (See "Resources" on page 126.) Check the system requirements of any program before you buy to make sure the software will run with your hardware.

Product	Number of Blocks Included	Appliqué Shapes	Key Features or Special Things You Can Do	Price*
Electric Quilt 4.1	Over 2,200	Yes	• Select a block from the library, or design your own • Rotate, recolor, and insert "real" fabric patterns into your blocks • Choose any layout, border style, and setting you can imagine • Create unique appliqué designs quickly and easily • Print out templates, appliqué patterns, foundations, yardage charts, and quilt layouts	$$$
Sew Precise! (Collections 1 and 2)	Over 1,100	No	• Foundation pattern program • Two collections of foundation-pieced blocks: New Inspirations (over 700 designs) and Old Favorites (over 350 designs) • Additional specialized collections available	$
Blockbase	Over 4,000	No	• CD-ROM version of Barbara Brackman's *Encyclopedia of Pieced Quilt Patterns* • Includes every pieced block published from 1835–1970 • Search for blocks several different ways • Print templates, foundations, or rotary cutting instructions in multiple sizes	$$
Quilt-Pro 3 (Available for both Windows and Macintosh)	Over 1,000	Yes	• Print templates, appliqué patterns, foundations, and yardage charts • Free demo available from Web site	$$
1-2-3 Quilt!	Over 500	No	• Easy to learn and use; perfect for computer novices • Traditional rotary-cut blocks • Step-by-step onscreen instructions • Library of digital fabric swatches from leading manufacturers; additional scans available free from Web site • Print rotary cutting charts, templates, foundations, and yardage charts • Free demo available from Web site • Upgrade available for advanced users	$

Which Software Is Right for Me?—continued

Product	Number of Blocks Included	Appliqué Shapes	Key Features or Special Things You Can Do	Price*
Foundation Factory	Over 500	No	• Foundation pattern program • Many special and designer editions available • Customize block size • Special bundled pricing available through Web site	$
PCQuilt (Limited version also available for Macintosh)	Over 100	Yes	• Design your own blocks • Create custom appliqué designs • Print templates, foundations, layouts, and yardage charts • Import fabric scans • Free demo available from Web site	$$
VQuilt	Over 300	No	• Simple to use, but capable of sophisticated designs • Draw freehand designs, including curves • Includes a library of 300 blocks and 68 quilts	$
QuiltSOFT 4.0	Over 300	No	• Calculates estimated yardage • Print templates • Can draw curves • Fabric collections available	$$

*Price: $ = under $50; $$ = $50 to $100; $$$ = over $100

Skill Builder

Create a library of fabrics in your computer.

STASH is a computer software program that will let you view thousands of fabric swatches from leading fabric manufacturers. During the design process, even when using paper and pencil, you can locate the perfect colors and fabric patterns. And if you're using design software, you'll be able to insert specific fabrics into your block and quilt designs. With STASH, you'll be able to audition designs that are close simulations of the final quilt and feel very confident when you're cutting up and sewing fabrics.

Try This!

Enjoy a free sample of computer designing.

If you're an old hand at designing on computer and you'd like to try creating more sophisticated designs, check this out. Without any purchase or obligation, you can download a 15-day trial drawing program from the Web. This preview lets you try Canvas, a design program (available for both Windows and Macintosh) that comes with a complete selection of drawing tools. Although it's not specific to quiltmaking, it can easily be used to create and print out intricate original designs.

Stars for *Stellar Quilts*

A quilt studded with Evening Stars abounds with universal appeal, whether it's a small charmer or a king-size bedcovering. In this chapter, quilter Elsie Campbell shows you how to draft any variation on this star block in a flash. Equally quick and easy are the lively Variable Star and the striking Fifty-Four Forty or Fight pattern. If you're up to the challenge of piecing diamonds, a LeMoyne Star, Lone Star, or Blazing Star may shine brighter for you. Pick a Star—the sky's the limit!

Getting Ready

From the simple Evening Star to the more complex Lone Star, star-patterned quilts are classic dazzlers. There are dozens of patterns for star blocks, and once you decide which star you like the best, the techniques in this chapter will help you draft it in any size with a minimum of effort. When you first begin drafting and constructing stars, pick a simple block, such as an Evening Star or Variable Star, then move on to more complex star blocks.

As you stargaze through this chapter, be aware that many of the blocks presented here are often known by different names. Evening Star, Variable Star, and Ohio Star have all been used for the same design, and Lone Star is often called Star of Bethlehem or Radiant Star. Just as you can pick your star pattern, you can choose the name you wish to use.

What You'll Need

¼" graph paper

Paper scissors

Mechanical pencil

Calculator

Metal ruler

Clear acrylic rulers:

   3" × 18" with ⅛" grid

   6" × 12" or 6" × 24" with 45° angle lines

Colored pencils

Protractor

Stars Based on a Nine-Patch Grid

Evening Star

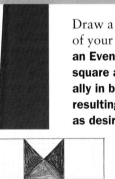

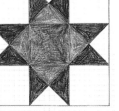

Draw a grid the desired finished size of your block (see page 14). **To draft an Evening Star, divide the middle square along each side in half diagonally in both directions. Color the resulting quarter-square triangles as desired to create star points.**

Eliminate the center square for a slightly different version of this star, as seen in the quilt on the opposite page ("Evening Star on the Farm"). See page 106 for instructions on rotary cutting the patches you draft or making templates.

For the Fifty-Four Forty or Fight block, draw a nine-patch grid your desired finished size. Measure and divide the center square and the four corner squares in half vertically and horizontally to make small Four Patch units. To draft the star points, **draw lines from the midpoint of each side of the center Four Patch to the outer corners** of the squares in the middle of each side. **Traditionally, these blocks have identically colored diagonal rows of small squares.**

Four-Patch Grid

Variable Star

Evening Star uses a 4 × 4 grid. Draw a square on graph paper the desired finished size of your block; measure and divide it into four rows of four squares.

For the star points, divide the two squares in the middle of each side in half diagonally, from the midpoint of the large center square out. **Color your star as desired. You can also divide the large center square into smaller squares or half-square triangles for additional design possibilities.**

LeMoyne Star

1

The LeMoyne Star (and similar eight-pointed stars) are not based on a grid. They are made of eight identical diamonds; you'll draft one diamond as a template. Using a 10-inch LeMoyne Star block as an example, begin by dividing the block size (10 inches) by 2, then divide that number by 2.41 (10 ÷ 2 = 5; 5 ÷ 2.41 = 2.07). Round that number to the nearest ⅛ inch— 2 inches, in this case. **Draw two parallel lines that distance apart on graph paper.**

Tip

Refer to "Decimal and Fraction Equivalents" on page 114 to round your number.

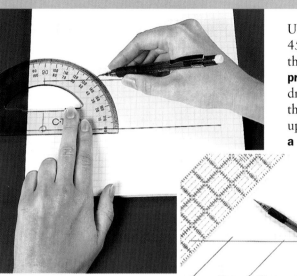

Use a protractor to locate and mark a 45-degree angle from the endpoint of the lower line. **Align the baseline of the protractor with the endpoint,** then draw a line from the endpoint through the marked point, to intersect with the upper line. **Use an acrylic ruler to draw a second line parallel to and 2 inches away from that angled line** (or the distance between the original lines), completing your diamond. This is your pattern for drafting eight identical star points. Add ¼-inch seam allowances around the outside to make a template or rotary cutting guide.

Tip

You could also use an acrylic ruler with a 45° angle line to measure and mark the angled side of the diamond.

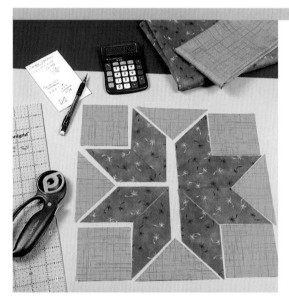

To complete the LeMoyne Star, you need **four corner squares and four side triangles.** For corner squares, multiply the width of the diamond star point by 1.41, then add ½ inch for seam allowances. In our example, $2 \times 1.41 = 2.82$ (round up to 2⅞); $2⅞ + ½ = 3⅜$ inches. Cut corner squares that size.

For setting triangles, multiply the finished width of the star point by 2, and add 1¼ inches for seam allowances. ($2 \times 2 = 4$; $4 + 1¼ = 5¼$ inches.) Cut one square that size, then cut it in half diagonally in both directions to yield four side triangles.

Tip

Cut corner squares and setting triangles a little larger than required. After you piece the block, you can then square it up and ensure perfect star points.

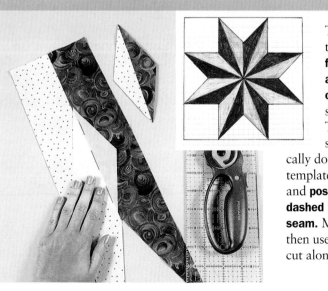

Try this LeMoyne Star design twist: **Use a light-color fabric for one side of each star point and a darker fabric for the other side.** This will give your star a three-dimensional look. To cut out the pieces for this star, draw a dashed line vertically down the middle of the original template. Prepare a two-color strip set, and **position the template so the dashed line falls exactly on the sewn seam.** Mark around the template, then use a ruler and rotary cutter to cut along the marked lines.

Carpenter's Star

1

The Carpenter's Star expands on the LeMoyne Star. You'll need 32 diamonds, 20 squares, and 8 side triangles. To size the diamonds, divide the block size (in this case, 12 inches) by 4, then divide that number by 2.41 (12 ÷ 4 = 3; 3 ÷ 2.41 = 1.245). Round that number to the nearest ¼ inch (1¼), then add ½ inch for seam allowances; draw and cut diamonds that are 1¾ inches. To size the corner squares and side triangles, see Step 3 on page 61.

2

Construction of this complicated-looking block is actually straightforward. First, arrange all the patches on a work surface or design wall as they will fall in the block. **Referring to the diagram,** sew the patches into numbered units 1 through 9; these units make up a quarter-block. Sew the units together in this order: 1 to 2; 3 and 5 to 4; 6 and 8 to 7. Sew 1-2 to 3-4-5; sew 6-7-8 to 9. Sew these two units together into a quarter-block. Repeat to make four quarter-blocks. Rotate the quarter-blocks to complete the arrangement, and join the quarters with set-in seams to complete the block.

Lone Star

The Lone Star is very similar to the LeMoyne Star. For the simplest Lone Star, first draft a LeMoyne Star (see page 60), then divide each diamond in half both ways. For quick piecing, cut strips of three different fabrics (strip width = width of small diamond + ½ inch). Make two different strip sets, and **cut them into 45-degree segments** the same width as the original strip. **Arrange the segments on a design wall;** then piece the star.

Blazing Star

The Blazing Star is a fun block to draft, and while it looks complicated, it ends up being a lot easier to piece than you might imagine. Begin by drawing a square the size of your desired finished block. **Draw straight lines dividing the block in half vertically, horizontally, and diagonally in both directions.**

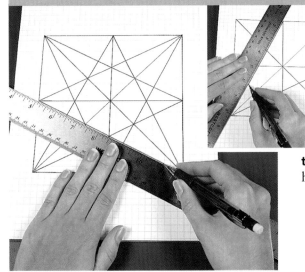

Start in any outer corner, and draw a line connecting the corner with the midpoint of one of the two sides opposite the corner. **Repeat from that corner to the other opposite side.**

Repeat with each of the three remaining corners until you have drawn eight angled lines.

Erase the lines inside the interior star to complete the Blazing Star pattern. Make reduced photocopies of the drafted star to audition various color and value schemes. Placing the darks and lights opposite each other in the inner and outer stars gives this star a sense of dimensionality. **Use only one color or fabric for the outer star to call more attention to the inner star,** but piece it the same as when using two fabrics.

Tip

Assemble each quadrant separately, in two triangular sections. Then sew the four quadrants together as you would a Four Patch.

STARS FOR STELLAR QUILTS

A Roundup
of Circle Patterns

Among the most well-loved of all traditional designs are those graced with circles and curves. Whether they're in vintage or contemporary quilts, patterns such as Drunkard's Path, Dresden Plate, Double Wedding Ring, and Wheel of Mystery (above) seem to universally capture the imaginations and admiration of quilters. These flowing patterns can be used as single, repeated blocks separated by sashing, or they can be set side by side to create the illusion of intertwined or continuous circles. From simple to complex, these designs are easy to draft, in any size. Follow Elsie Campbell's instructions, and give one a whirl!

Getting Ready

Curves and circles are really very easy to work with. Once you learn to draw a perfect circle, you'll be able to draft some ingenious designs, in exactly the size you want or need. The size of your desired pattern will help you determine what tools you need. For drafting very large patterns, look for rolls of butcher paper, newsprint, or even paper tablecloths at least 36 inches wide; they're generally fairly inexpensive at office, drafting, or party supply stores. No matter what the size of your pattern, make sure that any marking tool you use is sharp and that you place the point of your compass exactly at the location that will be the center of your arc or circle. When drawing any circle, remember that the size of your circle is the diameter, the measurement all the way across the center of the circle. When drawing a circle with a compass, you'll use half the diameter, or the radius, as the measurement for the span of the compass.

What You'll Need

- **Large paper, or sheets taped together**
- **Metal compass**
- **Yardstick compass**
- **Pencil**
- **String**
- **Pushpin**
- **Metal ruler**
- **Protractor**
- **Clear acrylic ruler, at least 3" wide**
- **Paper scissors**
- **Clear tape**

Drafting Circles

Using a Standard Compass

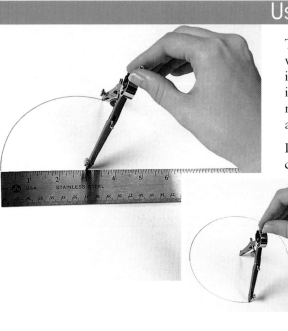

The simplest way to draw a circle is with a standard metal compass, which is reliable for drafting circles up to 6 inches in diameter. For greatest accuracy, use a compass with a crossbar and a small wheel between the arms.

Position the metal pivot point of the compass at the point that will be the center of the circle. **Hold the top of the compass and draw half the circle.** Without lifting the pivot point off the paper, lift the lead point and place it where you originally began, then **draw the remaining half of the circle in the opposite direction.**

Tip

If your pivot point slips while you draw, place a piece of cardboard or an old cutting mat underneath the paper.

65

For Bigger Circles

For circles larger than 6 inches, use a yardstick compass, which you can find in art and drafting supply shops. It consists of two clips (pivot point and lead point) that slip over any yardstick or ruler. Adjust the radius of your circle to any length on your ruler.

If you don't have a yardstick compass, tie a length of string around a pencil. Measure and place a pushpin through the string at the correct length for the pivot point. **Keep the string taut while drawing the circle.**

Quick & Dirty

For large circles that don't have to be absolutely precise, use this ruler and pencil method. Make a small X at the center of your circle. Hold the corner of a ruler at the X and make a tick mark at the measurement on the ruler that corresponds to the circle's radius. Shift the outer end of the ruler about 1 inch, being sure to keep the other end exactly at the X. **Keep shifting the ruler and making tick marks** until you complete the circle's perimeter. **Connect the dots with smooth, gently curved lines.**

Drunkard's Path

1

The Drunkard's Path block has an arc with its center at a corner of the block. **The proportions of the curved portion to the rest of the block can vary.** A two-thirds proportion is the most common.

Begin by drawing a square the size of your finished block. **Divide one side of the square into thirds by measuring and dividing the length by 3.** Mark off the side into thirds.

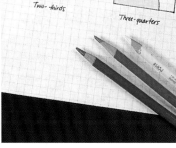

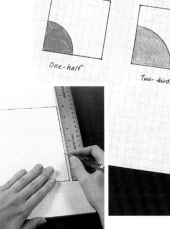

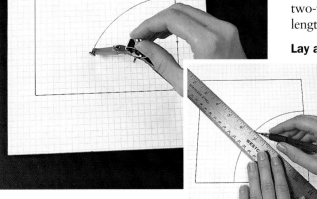

Place the metal pivot point of your compass at a corner of the block. Adjust the span of your compass so it is two-thirds of the block's length (or the length you have chosen). **Draw the arc.**

Lay a ruler from the corner where you placed the compass point to the opposite corner, and make a tick mark through the center of the arc. This mark will help you match your patches when piecing.

Use this drafted block to make templates for piecing. See page 107 for instructions.

Fan Blocks

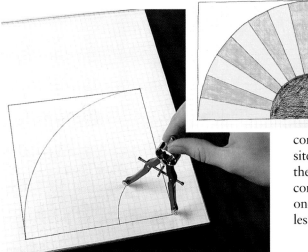

A Grandmother's Fan block consists of two arcs, between which are the fan "blades." To draft the block, draw a square the size of your finished block. Adjust your compass to the length of one side and draw an arc from one corner to the corner diagonally opposite, for the outer edge of the fan. For the inner edge of the fan, adjust the compass to a smaller radius (usually one-third the length of the side or less) **and draw a second arc.**

Tip

Piece the curved edges by hand (see page 29) or by machine (see page 110).

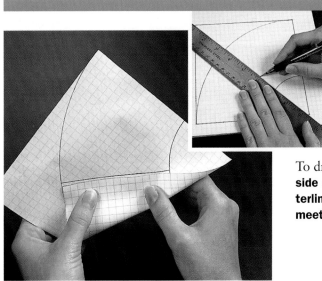

Position a ruler so it goes through the corner where you placed the compass point and the corner diagonally opposite. **Draw a pencil line from the inner arc to the outer one.** This is the centerline of your fan. Cut out the square.

To draw an eight-blade fan, **fold one side of the block in toward the centerline so that the edge of the square meets the centerline.** Crease the fold.

3

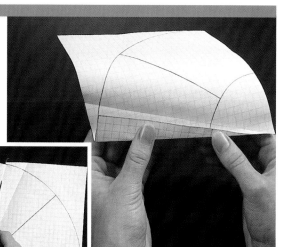

Tip

See page 107 for instructions on making templates, or page 108 to foundation-piece all the blades.

Open the fold, then **refold the edge of the block to meet the first crease.** Crease this new fold. The segment from the side of the block to the second crease is the pattern for one of the eight blades in the fan; **cut it out to make a template you can use for all the blades.** Use the drafted block to make additional templates for the fan center and background area. Remember to add seam allowances when cutting fabric pieces.

4

For a different number of fan blades, use a protractor. Align its baseline at the inside corner of your fan block. Divide the angle on the other outside edge (90 degrees, if it's a square block) by the number of blades you want. Here, 90 ÷ 5 = 18, so each blade will be 18 degrees. **Place small tick marks along the protractor at 18-degree intervals.** Then place a ruler at the inside corner of your fan and align it with each tick mark to **draw the dividing line for each of the blades.**

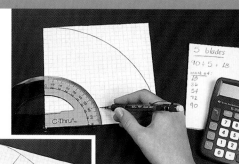

Dresden Plate

1

Decide on the approximate diameter of your finished Dresden Plate. Use a clear acrylic ruler to draw perpendicular lines at least as long as the desired diameter of your "plate." The intersection will be the center of your plate. Begin with two concentric circles (circles that share the same center point). Draw a large and a small circle, using the intersection of the lines as the center point for both. **Make the small inner circle about one-quarter to one-third the size of the large outer one.**

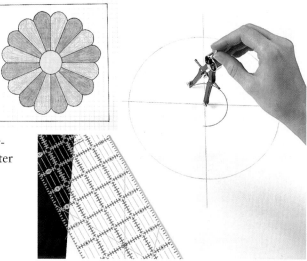

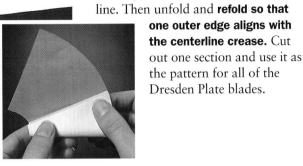

Cut out one-quarter of the pattern along the drawn lines. **Cut out the small, inner quarter-circle;** set it aside to use as a pattern for a template later. For a 16-blade Dresden Plate, carefully align the edges of the blade section, and crease to form the center-line. Then unfold and **refold so that one outer edge aligns with the centerline crease.** Cut out one section and use it as the pattern for all of the Dresden Plate blades.

Tip

To create another number of blades, refer to step 4 on the opposite page.

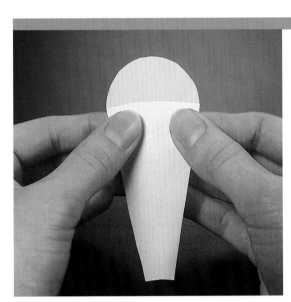

To create a scalloped edge, as shown at the bottom of the opposite page, measure across the wide end of the blade pattern. Draw and cut out a circle with that diameter (set your compass for half that measurement). **Position the blade on top of the circle so that the outer edges just touch.** Tape the circle to the blade to complete the pattern.

To add a pointed end to your blade pattern, fold the blade in half length-wise and crease the centerline. Then fold a small square of paper in half diagonally and crease it. **Nest the fold lines, with the square beneath the blade, and slide the square until its edges exactly meet the upper corners of the blade.** Tape them together and trim the protruding corners of the square to **complete the pattern for a Dresden Plate with a pointed edge.**

Tip

Piece the blades together by machine. Then appliqué the pieced unit to the background.

A ROUNDUP OF CIRCLE PATTERNS

Secondary Circle Patterns

There are many popular quilt patterns based on circles. Often, each individual block contains only a portion of a circle (an arc). When you place the blocks in a side-by-side set, though, you'll see a secondary pattern emerge—a whole circle. Here are several blocks that use arcs to create secondary circular designs.

If you have any trouble drafting one of these designs, you might want to start with an easy exercise. Photocopy the diagram (black and white is fine), enlarging the design by 200 percent. Following the directions, use a compass to go over the arcs and circles, tracing the design on top of the lines shown. When you feel comfortable with the process, try drafting the pattern on another sheet of paper, creating a block or four-block set in a different size.

When you are ready to move from a drafted design to fabric, pay close attention to the tips for curved piecing on page 110. Pieced arcs, like the wedges of the Double Wedding Ring and the zigzag along the narrow arc of Buggy Wheel, are easily and accurately assembled using foundation piecing (see page 108).

Orange Peel

This Orange Peel block, also known as Tea Leaf and Lover's Knot, is based on a 4 × 4 grid. The design is created by overlapping curves. Set your compass to a radius equal to the length of one grid unit. Begin at the center of one quadrant; draw a circle. Repeat in each of the quadrants, then add a circle in the center. The green dots on the diagram indicate compass pivot points. Move your compass to each remaining point to draw arcs as needed to complete the design. Your pattern will quickly emerge as you move along the outer edges of the square.

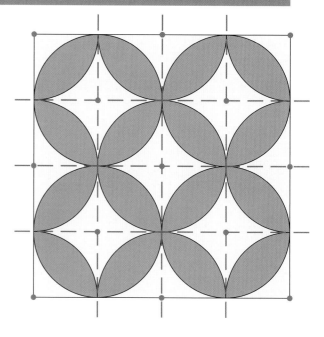

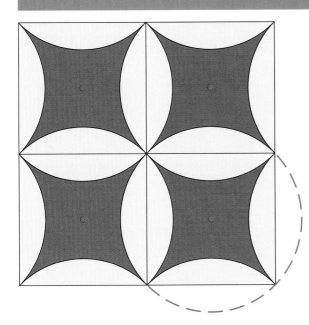

This pattern is called Trey's Quilt. The radius of the circle needed to draw the arcs is equal to one-half the diagonal measurement of one square of this Four Patch block. Place your compass point at the center of each Four Patch block (as shown by the green dots) and draw your circles. You will need to repeat the grid beyond the intended design in order to provide compass pivot points for all the arcs within the design area.

Wheel of Mystery

While the Wheel of Mystery pattern may look complicated and mysterious, it's fairly easy to draft. Draw a grid of nine squares that are each the finished block size. (You may need to tape pieces of graph paper together, and you may also need a yardstick compass if your compass span is smaller than the block size.) Find the center point of each of the nine squares and mark it. Set a compass to span the length of one side of your finished-size block. Place the compass point at the center of the center square, shown here with a green dot, and draw a full circle, as shown in red. Repeat for each of the remaining eight squares. Use the center square in your grid as a pattern to make the three templates: a clover leaf petal, a corner piece, and a curved triangle.

Color and fabric choices can create stunning effects, as evidenced by Brooke Flynn's Sunset Wheel of Mystery, shown here and on pages 2–3 and 64.

To piece this block, stitch a corner to each petal. Stitch a curved triangle between two of these units to create one section; make a second section in the same way. Stitch the remaining curved triangles to one of these sections, then sew that to the other section in one continuous, curved seam.

Tip

The trick to piecing this design successfully is to press the seams either open or in a rotation, so as to distribute the bulk evenly.

A ROUNDUP OF CIRCLE PATTERNS

Double Wedding Ring

The Double Wedding Ring is fairly simple to draw when broken down into components—overlapping concentric circles. The center point of the main ring in each block is the center point of that block. Set four blocks together to draw the overlapping circles. Their centers are the corners of the blocks. Draw all the outer edges of the rings first, setting your compass radius to one-half the measurement of a side of one block. Then adjust your compass slightly smaller as desired, and draw all the inner circles. Use the folding technique described on pages 67–68 or a protractor (page 68) to divide each arc into six equal sections. (The "corners" of each arc are already drawn by the intersecting arcs.)

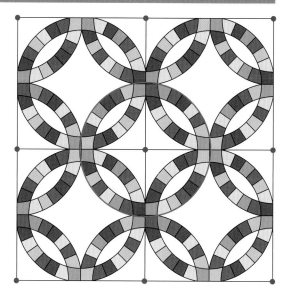

Buggy Wheel

This Buggy Wheel (or Wheel of Fortune) is another wonderful pattern based on arcs. To draw the concentric arcs in each corner, set your compass radius to one-half the measurement of the side of one block, and draw all the large arcs first to keep them the exact same size. Then decrease the compass arc and draw the next set of arcs, and again for the smallest arcs. To form the little sawtooth triangles, use the protractor technique on page 68 to divide the outer two arcs into twelve equal sections, then draw a zigzag line between divisions on the smaller and larger arcs. To draw the inner square, draw diagonal guidelines (see the green dashed lines) and connect the points where the diagonals intersect with the outermost arc.

The Quilter's
Problem Solver

Smooth Curves Ahead

Problem

My curved seams aren't smooth.

Solution

Try one or more of these suggestions.

❏ Make sure your stitch length is set to 16 stitches per inch (or more, depending on your machine). Since the actual stitches are straight, not curved, your curved seam is actually a series of small, straight lines. The shorter the better, and the smoother your sewn curve will be.

❏ After stitching but before pressing, clip into the seam allowances along curves, stopping a couple of threads before the stitching. This will allow the curve to lie flatter when you press. Clip at frequent intervals along tight curves.

❏ Set your seam before sewing. Press the seam as it was sewn, without opening out either fabric. This helps the seam lie more smoothly.

❏ Try pressing in the other direction. If your pressed seam doesn't lie flat, re-set the seam and press it again, sending the seam allowance toward the other fabric. If you're concerned about the darker fabric showing through, trim the seam allowances so the darker fabric is slightly narrower than the lighter one.

Skill Builder

Hide that imperfect seam under the couch.

To hide or cover a curved seam that just doesn't pass muster, try disguising it with a decorative embellishment. Lay a contrasting or coordinating color of ribbon, decorative thread, or even lace along the seam. Then couch it in place using a zigzag stitch and either matching thread or clear monofilament.

Try This!

Mimic curved piecing with appliqué.

If you love the look of these circular patterns but haven't yet gotten the courage to piece one, no problem. Cut the pieces out of your chosen fabrics at the finished size—with no seam allowances—and appliqué them onto the background. For a crisp look, press fusible web to the back of the fabrics before cutting out the curved shapes. Fuse the pieces to the background, then machine sew around the edges. You can use a blindstitch in matching thread or a decorative stitch in contrasting thread. Alternately, consider an interesting raw-edge texture: skip the fusible, pin or glue-baste the pieces in place, and topstitch the edges with matching or contrasting thread.

Starting from
a Circle

Going in circles can be a creative process when you're using a circle as the starting point for drafting. Amazingly, from a humble circle, you can create all kinds of triangles, diamonds, hexagons, octagons, and five-pointed stars quickly and easily, and in any size you want. You'll be delighted with the design possibilities that open up to you. Learn the secrets here from Elsie Campbell, and join the "inner circle" of quilters who draft their own designs.

Getting Ready

Drafting from a circle is cool and fun. The circle method is quick and exact, and it lets you draft triangles and hexagons in an infinite number of sizes, not just in lengths that are easy to measure. As for 5-pointed stars and pentagons, there may not be another way to draft them perfectly.

Be aware that any slight shift in the position of your compass can throw off your circle, your measurements, and the shapes that come out of them. Avoid errors by ensuring that your compass point stays exactly where it's supposed to, and your circles and arcs will be precise and consistent. Try placing an old cutting mat underneath your paper; the compass point will sink in just enough to keep it in place and guard against slippage. Or use a piece of cardboard from the back of a legal pad. Both of these also protect the rest of the pad of paper from holes where the compass point pokes through.

For a variety of techniques for drawing circles that range in size from tiny to tremendous, see "A Roundup of Circle Patterns" on page 64.

What You'll Need

Paper

Compass

Metal, cork-backed ruler

Mechanical pencil

Clear acrylic ruler with 45° angle lines

Paper scissors

Equilateral Triangle

1

An equilateral triangle has three equal sides and three 60-degree angles. Quilt blocks like Joseph's Coat, Streak o' Lightning, and Thousand Pyramids include this shape. Set your compass so it spans the desired finished length of a side of your triangle; **draw a circle with that radius.** Label the center point A.

Tip

Length of an equilateral triangle's side = radius of the circle.

2

Use a ruler to draw a line connecting the exact center of the circle (point A) with any point on the circle. Label the point where your line intersects the circle B. Keeping the compass set to the same length, **place the point of the compass at point B and draw an arc that intersects the circle.** Label this new intersection point C.

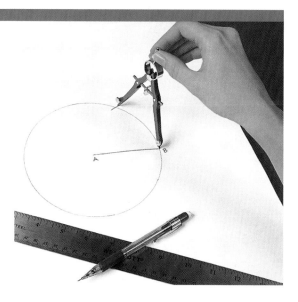

3

Using a ruler, draw a straight line connecting points B and C. To complete the triangle, **draw a third straight line from point C to point A.** Use this pattern to make your templates for tracing or piecing an equilateral triangle.

60-Degree Diamond

From the equilateral triangle, it's a simple matter to make a 60-degree diamond. Place the compass point on point C, and draw another arc intersecting the circle. Label this point D. **Connect point D with points A and C to complete the diamond.** Erase the line (AC) that crosses through the center of your completed diamond. Use this shape for Baby Blocks, Seven Sisters, or any other six-pointed star designs.

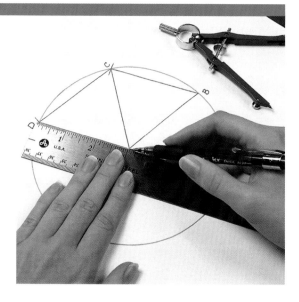

Hexagon

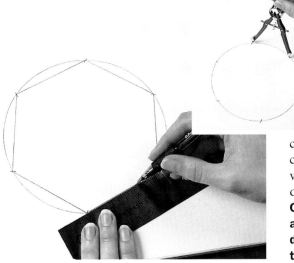

To make a hexagon, set your compass for a radius that's half the width of the hexagon you want, and draw a circle. Then, with the compass still set at the same span, place the point anywhere on the drawn circle and draw an arc that crosses the circle. Move the compass to the point where the arc intersects the circle and draw another arc along the circle. **Continue repositioning and drawing arcs all the way around. Use a ruler to draw lines that connect the intersections to make a perfect hexagon.**

Length of a hexagon's side = radius of the circle.

Octagon

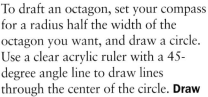

To draft an octagon, set your compass for a radius half the width of the octagon you want, and draw a circle. Use a clear acrylic ruler with a 45-degree angle line to draw lines through the center of the circle. **Draw two perpendicular lines first, then two at 45 degrees to the first two lines.**

As an alternative, cut out the circle and **fold it into eight equal "pie wedges."** Fold the circle in half, then again into quarters, then into eighths; unfold.

Length of an octagon's side = ¾ the radius of the circle.

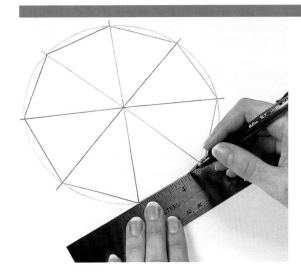

Connect the points where the lines (or creases) intersect with the outer edge of the circle, and voilà! You've drafted a perfect octagon. Use the octagon to draft and piece block patterns such as Spider Web or Snowball.

Extend all the straight lines along the sides of a hexagon or octagon to form six- or eight-pointed stars.

Five-Pointed Stars

1

Perfect five-pointed stars are a classic appliqué motif. **They can add a little sparkle to the open areas of a patchwork quilt or provide snappy folk art accents to a landscape or baby quilt.** If you've ever wondered how to draft a perfect star, wonder no more. All it takes is a compass, a ruler, and a little practice.

2

Draw a circle, then draw two perpendicular lines through the center point. Locate the midpoint of one radius: Slightly decrease the span of your compass. Place the compass point where the radius intersects the circle; draw short arcs above and below the radius. Keeping the same span, place the compass point at the center of the circle; **draw arcs to intersect with the previous ones. Then, line up a ruler with the two intersections and mark the point where the ruler crosses the radius** (the exact midpoint); label it A.

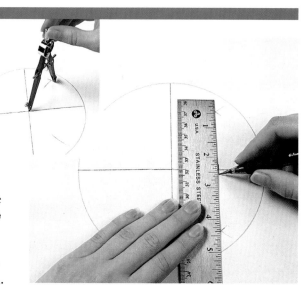

3

Label the intersection of the adjacent radius and the top of the circle B. Place the point of the compass at point A and **adjust the compass until the pencil point is exactly at B.** Then, without moving the point of the compass, **draw an arc through the left horizontal radius.** Label the point where this new arc intersects the radius C.

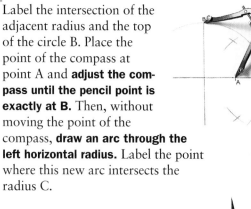

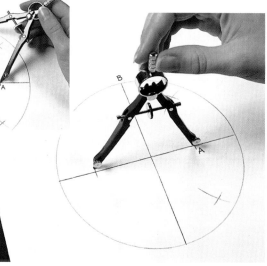

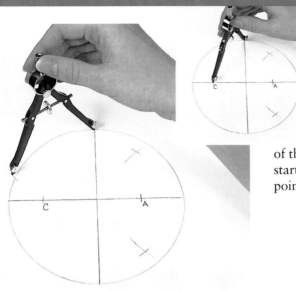

4

Place the point of the compass at B. **Adjust the compass until the pencil point is exactly at C.** Then, without moving the point of the compass, **draw an arc through the outer edge of the circle.** The intersection of this arc and the circle will be the starting point for marking off the five points of your star.

5

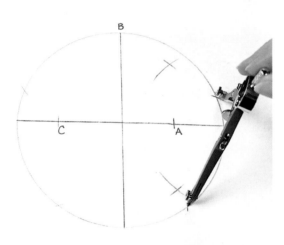

Keeping the compass set at the same span, place the compass point on the intersection, draw an arc that intersects the circle, and then move the point of the compass to this new intersection to draw another arc. Continue repositioning the compass point, working your way around the circle and drawing arcs, until you **divide the circle into five equal parts.**

6

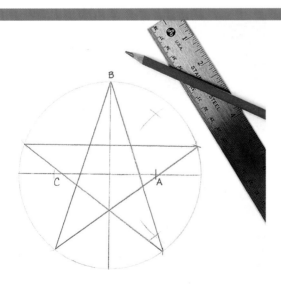

Each intersection of an arc with the circle's perimeter is a point of your star. **Use a ruler to connect every other intersection to draw a five-pointed star.** Use this pattern as a template to trace or cut stars; remember to add seam allowances before cutting shapes from fabric. If you prefer to piece your star instead, make a pentagon template for the center and a triangle template to use for all five points of the star.

Your Very Own
Mariner's Compass

The Mariner's Compass is one of the most impressive and challenging quilt designs, from drafting it on paper to piecing it in fabric. But don't be intimidated! You can navigate uncharted waters and learn the drafting process by following Karen Kay Buckley's step-by-step instructions. Then you'll see how the Mariner's Compass breaks down into identical small sections that make the piecing process easier to maneuver. So ship out on one of your greatest quilting adventures and draft one today!

Getting Ready

Drafting the Mariner's Compass depends as much on the precision of your tools as it does on your ability to follow directions. Make sure all your pencil points (including the lead in your compass) are *sharp*. You'll need precise, crisp lines to draft and piece accurately.

Decide how large you want your Mariner's Compass to be, and then choose the appropriate method for drafting a circle of that size. A standard (sometimes called student) metal compass will draft circles up to 12 inches across, depending on the compass. For larger circles, use a yardstick compass. (See pages 12 and 66 to see these clip-on attachments and learn how to use them.)

In this chapter, we show the drawn lines in different colors so that it's easy to refer from the text to the photos and to see what's being drawn in each step. You may prefer to draw your Mariner's Compass in only one color.

What You'll Need

Large paper, or sheets taped together

Sharp pencil

Clear acrylic rulers:

   12" or 15" square

   3" × 18"

Metal, cork-backed ruler or yardstick

Metal compass or yardstick compass

Colored pencils (optional)

Drafting the Mariner's Compass

1

Decide what size you want your finished quilt block to be. **Draw a square that size on plain paper.** If you have a large square acrylic ruler, use it to complete this step easily and accurately.

It's best to start with a larger square, at least 10 × 10 inches, such as the one shown here. It's easier to work in a larger format when you're getting acquainted with this complex design.

2

Draw horizontal and vertical lines to divide the square in half. Where these lines cross is the exact center of the square and of your Mariner's Compass. **Then, lay a long ruler from corner to opposite corner and draw diagonal lines in both directions.** These lines, which also intersect at the exact center of the block, will be your guidelines for drafting, although you will not use them for piecing.

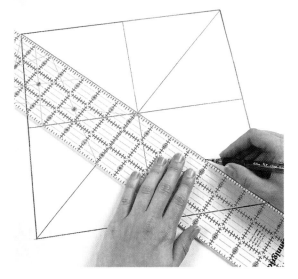

3

To create the outer finished edge of your Mariner's Compass, **draw a large circle.** Place the point of your compass on the exact center of your block, and open the compass so it draws a circle at least ¼ inch inside the drawn square (to avoid problems when you piece or appliqué the edges of the Mariner's Compass).

4

Draw another, smaller circle inside the outer circle. The size of this circle determines the look of your Mariner's Compass. **A large inner circle will give you short, fat rays, while a small inner circle will make long, thin rays.** Decide on the look you want and use the compass to draw this inner circle, placing the point of the compass at the exact center of the design.

5

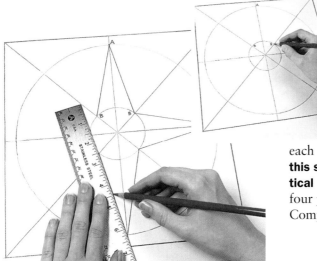

Find the point where the vertical line intersects the outer circle. Label it A. Find the points where the adjacent diagonal lines intersect the inner circle. **Label the two points B.**

Draw a line from point A to each point B to make one ray. **Repeat this step at each horizontal and vertical line** and you will have the first four primary rays of your Mariner's Compass.

Tip

These first four rays are the North, South, East, and West "directionals" of your Mariner's Compass.

6

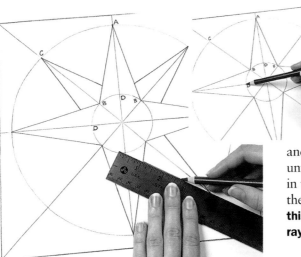

Find the point where one diagonal line intersects the outer circle. Label it C. Find the points where the adjacent straight lines intersect the inner circle. **Label the two points D.**

Align the ruler with point C and a point D; draw from C toward D until you reach a line AB. Draw a line in the same way on the other side of the diagonal to complete a ray. **Repeat this step to create the four secondary rays of your Mariner's Compass.**

Tip

Continue the lines from C all the way to D to create a small, eight-pointed star around the center circle (see the quilts on pages 80 and 85).

7

Find the inner point (between two rays) where line AB intersects line CD. **Label this point E.**

Align the edge of your long ruler with the exact center of the block and point E. The ruler should cross both sides of the outer circle. **Make four small tick marks where the ruler crosses the inner and outer circles.** Repeat this step at each of the three additional inner point (E) intersections to draw a total of 16 tick marks.

YOUR VERY OWN MARINER'S COMPASS

8

Choose any tick mark on the outer circle. **Label it F.** Find the tick marks to the left and right of point F on the inner circle. **Label these G.**

Align your ruler so it passes through point F and one point G. Draw a line from point F toward G, but stop at the first line you reach. Repeat with the point G on the other side of the same point F. **Make a total of eight tertiary rays in this manner, starting from each point F on the outer circle.**

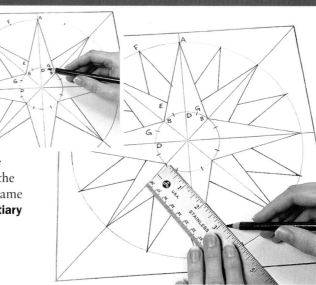

9

To construct the standard Mariner's Compass, refer to page 107 for instructions on making templates. **Make one template each for pieces A, B, C, D, and E** (or make individual freezer paper templates for every piece in the compass). Note that the D pieces will form the background for the compass.

If, in Step 6, you continued your lines to the center circle and you are creating a Mariner's Compass variation with an eight-pointed star around the center, **make a template for A1** and use it in combination with a B template, in place of A.

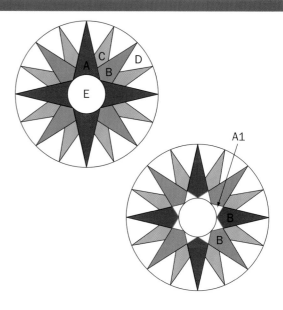

10

Tip

If your templates are finished size, remember to add ¼" seam allowances when cutting your patches from fabric.

For the standard Mariner's Compass, cut four A pieces from your primary ray fabric and four B pieces from the secondary ray fabric.

For the Mariner's Compass variation with the eight-pointed star in the center, cut eight A1 pieces from your chosen star fabric. Cut four B rays from the fabric you chose for the primary rays of your compass, then sew an A1 piece to either side of your primary B rays. Also cut four B rays from the fabric you chose for the secondary rays.

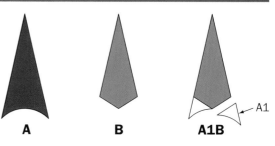

84

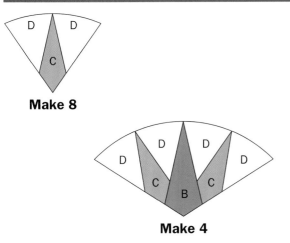

Make 8

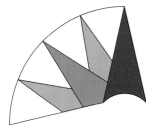

Make 4

Cut 16 D pieces from your background fabric. Also cut 8 C pieces from the fabric you have chosen for your tertiary rays. **You are now ready to begin assembling your Mariner's Compass:** Sew a D background piece to each side of each of your tertiary C pieces to make a total of eight DCD units. Press the seam allowances toward the background fabric. Then sew a DCD unit to each side of each B (secondary) ray. Press the seam allowances toward the background fabric.

Tip

If you wish to exclude the tertiary rays on your Mariner's Compass variation, you'll need a background piece for each D-C-D area.

Make 4

Make 4

Assemble your Mariner's Compass in four quadrants. **Prepare each quadrant of the design as follows:** Sew each BCD unit to the left side of an A (primary) ray. (If you are making an eight-pointed center star, sew each BCD unit to an A1B unit.) Make a total of four of these units. Press the seam allowances toward the background fabric.

Sew these four units together, pressing the seam allowances toward the background fabric. Sew the complete compass to the center E circle. Press the seam allowances toward the center circle, clipping into the seam allowance so it lies flat.

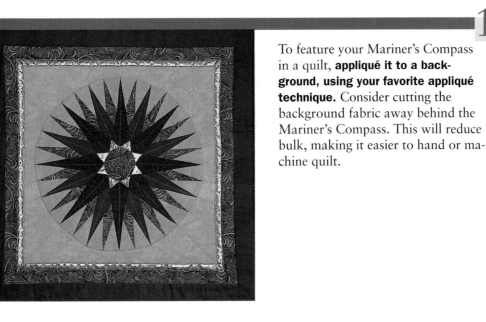

To feature your Mariner's Compass in a quilt, **appliqué it to a background, using your favorite appliqué technique.** Consider cutting the background fabric away behind the Mariner's Compass. This will reduce bulk, making it easier to hand or machine quilt.

Tip

Quilt along the center of each ray, extending the lines outward so your Mariner's Compass radiates.

Flying Geese
in Free-Form Flight

The traditional Flying Geese quilt pattern has rows of straight triangles that mimic the flight of migrating birds. Although real geese usually fly in formations, their flight plans are not strictly in straight lines. And each goose is not an exact replica of another. Mimic their meandering journeys and their unique qualities by giving them a curved formation and a dash of individuality as Caryl Bryer Fallert does in her stunning quilts. With these instructions for free-form variations from Elsie Campbell, the time is right for your next quilt to take wing.

Getting Ready

The traditional Flying Geese pattern has strict proportions and rigid angles (see "Anatomy of a Goose" below). When you draw your curved Flying Geese, maintaining approximately the same proportion of goose to background will make your design more recognizable. However, if you're looking for something more modern, you can vary the sizes and angles to your heart's content. There are several variations described in this chapter. Use them in different combinations for as raucous a gaggle of geese as you'd like.

Most people can successfully draw freehand curves with a little practice, but if you're not confident in your ability to draw smooth curved lines or you want more control and evenness, the Flexicurve tool (shown on page 88) is available at most quilt shops and drafting stores.

Curved Flying Geese are most successfully pieced using a foundation; see page 108 for instructions and tips.

Breaking Formation

Anatomy of a Goose

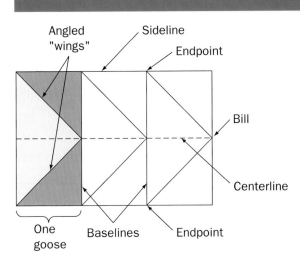

The traditional Flying Geese block is based on a rectangle that's twice as wide as it is tall. Each long edge is the baseline for one "goose." Angled "wing" lines connect the endpoints of one baseline with the center of the next goose; the point where the wing lines meet is the goose's "bill." The short sides of the rectangles make up the sidelines, and the line (sometimes imaginary) that runs through each bill is the centerline.

Practicing Curves

The first thing you'll need to do when drafting a strip of curved Flying Geese is to **practice drawing curves.** This may seem simple, but it's important to remember that you'll be sewing along the curved lines that you draw, so draw gentle, flowing curves. Avoid sharp turns; they'll be trouble when it comes time to sew your design into fabric. **If you're unsure of the steadiness of your hand, use a Flexicurve tool to help you get the exact curve you want.** Simply shape it as desired, then draw along the edge.

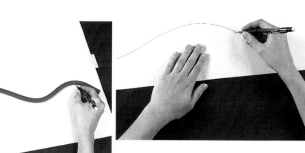

Drawing "Standard" Curved Geese

1

To draft a strip of curved geese, draw two curved sidelines, about the same distance apart along their length. This distance is the finished strip width. Use a ruler to **draw straight baselines from one sideline to the other.** For "traditional" geese, space the baselines evenly, about one-half the width of the strip apart.

To position the bills, **draw a gently curved centerline about halfway between the two sidelines** for the entire length. The geese will follow one another in a flowing line.

2

To draw the angled wings, use a ruler to **draw lines from the endpoints of each baseline to the intersection of the centerline and the baseline above.** When you color in the geese (the triangular shapes formed by the wings and the baseline), **the wings will pop out from the background.**

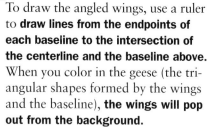

Shifting the Baseline

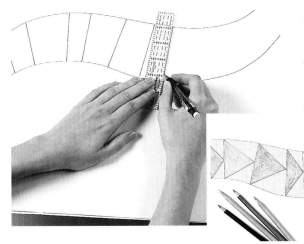

Once you master drafting the basic curved goose, give each goose a little "personality," starting with size differences. **Draw in baselines, spacing them at different intervals.**

This will yield **some fatter geese and some skinnier ones.** Keeping the centerline approximately halfway between the sidelines aligns the bills along the curve.

Don't make the baselines too close together. Remember that you'll have to piece geese between them, so make them at least an inch apart.

For another baseline variation, let each goose fly according to its own internal compass. Instead of making the baselines perpendicular to the sidelines, **draw each baseline at a different angle. This will produce a strip of geese that seem to tilt and tip their wings in all directions.** Watch for any geese that are too sharply angled to be easily pieced, and redraw their baselines. A centerline midway between the sidelines, as shown, helps keep these "off-balance" geese flying as a group.

Swerving the Centerline

For geese that dip and swoop in their line formation, **let the centerline meander from side to side,** drawing it so it first curves closer to one sideline, then approaches the opposite one. The geese will still "follow" one another, since all their bills will be along a single line, **but each goose keeps its unique look.**

For Flying Geese that fly off into the distance, gradually draw the sidelines closer to each other as you near the end of your strip of geese.

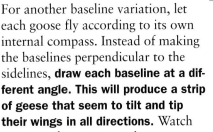

FLYING GEESE IN FREE-FORM FLIGHT

2

If the geese in your imagined design don't exactly follow the leader, show this by changing the bill placement from goose to goose. Instead of drawing a continuous centerline, draw a dot or tick mark in a random position on each baseline (except the very bottom one). **Draw your angled wings** from the endpoints of the baseline to the dot on the next baseline; **your gaggle of geese will seem to be flocking to points all over the globe!**

Combining Drafting Tricks

1

When you mingle baseline and centerline options, you can achieve many different looks. Start with the more traditional patterns and work your way up to more out-of-the-ordinary combinations as you grow more confident in both drafting and piecing. **Try your designs on paper in a small scale first to see which ones you like.** Use colored pencils to represent fabrics or values.

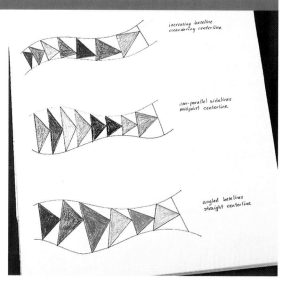

2

As long as you can piece your strip, you can make it as nontraditional as you like. **Vary everything—strip width, baseline height, wing angles, bill placement.** What you get may end up looking less like Flying Geese and more like an abstract work of art, but who says they have to look like geese, anyway?

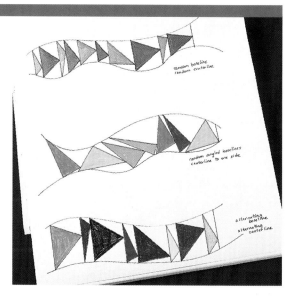

Tip

Consider an overall pattern for an innovative quilt: rows of nested curves, each featuring a gaggle of geese drafted with lots of variety.

Translations in Fabric

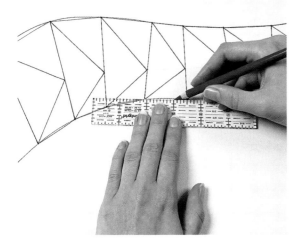

If you like the curved look but don't want to sew curved seams, you can mimic the curves but still sew straight lines. Draw curved geese in the style you like, choosing from one on the previous pages or designing your own. Then, **use a small ruler to connect the endpoints of each baseline with the one above it,** drawing over the curves with short, straight segments. Your design will give the illusion of being curved, aided by the short, straight lines.

Tip

The shorter your straight lines are, the more they will give the illusion of a smooth curve; longer segments will appear more angled.

Pictorial shapes and special fabrics can provide inspiration for curved Flying Geese designs. As seen in Caryl Bryer Fallert's quilt on page 86, curved Flying Geese strips complement both the graceful silhouette appliqués and the beautiful background of hand-dyed fabric. Ocean prints can inspire appliquéd starfish or clamshells; Flying Geese strips might serve as the edge of the sea. **Or create a scene from outer space with Flying Geese rocket trails in fiery colors against a background of celestial print fabric.**

Sometimes a quilt with wide borders needs something to make it more exciting. **Consider incorporating curved Flying Geese strips into your borders.** Sew a strip in the colors, design, and size you want. Then, pin it in place on the border. Appliqué it using your favorite technique (see pages 112–13), and your quilt has a whole new area of interest!

Tip

Embellish the edges of your appliquéd border with a decorative machine stitch. Featherstitch would be most appropriate!

FLYING GEESE IN FREE-FORM FLIGHT

Drafting
Pineapples

The pieced Pineapple pattern has long been a favorite among quilters. Because it grew out of the Log Cabin block, it's sometimes called a Pineapple Log Cabin. Strips surround the center square as in a regular Log Cabin, but instead of just four strips around the sides of a center square, the Pineapple adds four diagonal strips so each "round" contains eight strips. While this may seem complex, it's a cinch to draft and piece. Dixie Haywood, who has won many awards for her Pineapple quilts, shares her know-how and her secrets for developing lots of fruitful variations.

Getting Ready

Decide what size block you wish to draft. The Pineapple is easiest to draft as a multiple of three: Try a 6-, 9-, or 12-inch block. Once you understand the basic drafting principles, you can easily adapt the technique to draft other sizes and alter the design.

For clarity, we drew our lines in different colors; you can draw all your lines with lead pencil. Clear acrylic rulers make it easy to ensure that lines are perpendicular, but you will also want to rely on the lines on graph paper for proper alignment and precise corners.

You can also use a computer program to draft the Pineapple block. (Refer to "Creating on the Computer" on page 48.) When drafting Pineapple blocks, set your software to use a 48 by 48 grid.

After you design your block, see page 106 for help with cutting and piecing.

What You'll Need

¼" graph paper

Clear acrylic rulers:

 3" × 18"

 1" × 6"

Mechanical pencil or pencil with a very sharp point

Eraser

Colored pencils

Fine-point permanent marker (optional)

Drafting Your Pineapple Block

On graph paper, draw a square the size of your finished Pineapple block. Using the ruler and the lines on the graph paper, **draw lines through the center of the square horizontally, vertically, and diagonally in both directions.**

2

Tip

For 6" blocks, mark off every ½"; for 12" blocks, mark off every 1".

Draft six concentric squares within your block. To do this, first divide the length of one side of your block by 2. Then divide that number by 6, and use the resulting number as an increment for **marking off tick marks along each of the horizontal and vertical lines.** In this 9-inch square block, half the block is 4½ inches; 4½ divided by 6 is ¾, so a tick mark is drawn every ¾ inch along each of these lines. Position the ruler about 1/16 inch below but parallel to the line, so each tick mark crosses the line.

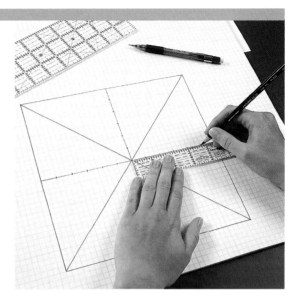

3

Use the tick marks and the lines on the graph paper to **draw concentric squares around the center of the block.** You should have one center square and five square "rings" surrounding it. The finished size of the center square is twice the finished width of the strips in the square rings.

4

Use a ruler and pencil to **draw an on-point square around the center square,** as shown in red. Draw this on-point square so that its corners meet at the original horizontal and vertical lines at the intersections of the next square ring. The midpoint of each side should touch a corner of the center square.

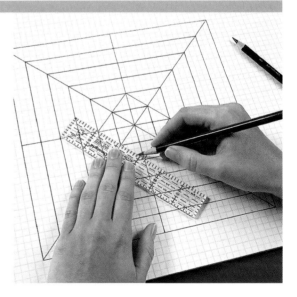

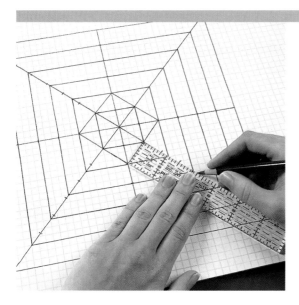

Working outward from the side of the on-point square, **measure and draw five tick marks along each diagonal line.** Use the same increment that you calculated in Step 2 (here, the increment is ¾ inch). Mark *only* five ticks; leave empty spaces in the corners.

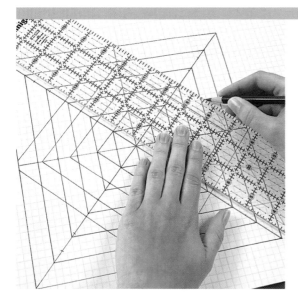

Using a ruler and the tick marks along the diagonal lines, **draw five sets of lines parallel to the center on-point square.** The corners of the squares meet at the horizontal and vertical lines. The first two sets will make complete square rings around the on-point square, but the remaining three rings would extend beyond the block, so theses lines will end at the sides of the block. Note that the distance from the last line to the corner will be wider than the distance between the other lines.

Tip

To ensure that the lines are parallel, use your clear acrylic ruler and align a printed line with a diagonal line before you draw.

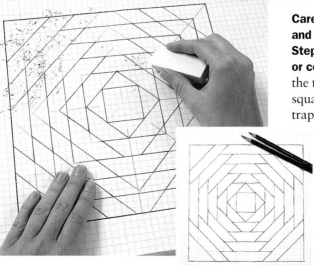

Carefully erase the vertical, horizontal, and diagonal lines that you drew in Step 1. Also erase all the right angles or corners that you drew, except for the two center squares. The center square, the center on-point square, the trapezoids, and the four corner triangles make up your complete drafted Pineapple block.

If you used different colors for drafting or if your lines are light, you may want to **trace or redraw the block with a fine-point permanent marker.** Make photocopies so you can try various color combinations later.

Tip

Check for precision: Fold the pattern in half horizontally on a light box to make sure the drawn lines are aligned. Refold it vertically and on each diagonal, too.

DRAFTING PINEAPPLES

Combining Blocks

Tip

Quilt a pattern
of concentric
circles to
further
emphasize the
intersections
of blocks,
rather than
the centers of
the blocks.

Wherever four Pineapple blocks come together, the four corner triangles create a diamond (on-point square). This presents an opportunity for endless creative designs. In Dixie Haywood's wonderful scrap quilt Memories, **the use of color and fabric play up these intersections between blocks.** By using similarly colored fabrics at these intersections, the design created by the four blocks, rather than the individual blocks, becomes the focus.

Echoed Shapes

Tip

Spotlight a
favorite fabric
in the larger
center
squares.

1

To experiment with design possibilities, start with a basic drafting of the Pineapple block in a four-block set. Change one element, and you will create a different look. Here's a way to feature the center of each block more prominently and echo the diamond (the square on-point shape that occurs where the corners of four blocks come together). **Erase or ignore the smaller center square.**

2

To inject a dash of an accent color, **add a smaller on-point square inside the center square of each individual block.** Simply connect the midpoints of each side of the center square to draw your new smaller center. In this variation, an additional diagonal line was drawn in each corner of the original block. This reduces the impact of the area where four blocks come together. Otherwise, the intersections could overwhelm the accent color in the smaller center on-point square.

Enlarging the corners of the Pineapple block is a great way to display a special large-print fabric or border print. To create a bigger corner, erase the outermost corner line. **Use two mirrors placed at 90-degree angles to each other to audition different areas of fabrics for these corner pieces.** When you set four blocks together, your choice of fabrics can create a kaleidoscope effect where the four patches join at the center.

Trace your pattern onto foundation paper or tear-away stabilizer to make piecing easy and precise (see page 108).

Accent Strips

You can also alter a Pineapple pattern by adding narrow accent lines. For example, **draw a line ¼ inch inside the triangle's base in each corner of each Pineapple block.** Use a clear acrylic ruler to draw lines exactly parallel to the original ones. Don't forget the ones at the center of the four-block set.

Tip

Play with your original block and vary the width of any strip or several strips to achieve different effects.

Experiment with using contrasting colors for this accent strip. In this block, **bright yellow sets off the center diamond in the four-block set.** Ignoring the center square in each block creates a visually pleasing echo of the diamond shapes created by the accent strips at the block intersections.

Color Variations

Alternating colors or values on the diagonals radiating out from the center creates an effect of ever-widening stripes that almost pulsate out to the corners. Using similar colors can make the pattern crisp and neat; contrasting colors will vibrate with energy.

Tip

Cut and paste fabric swatches onto cardboard to make a sample block before you cut the pieces for an entire quilt.

Using the same fabric for the entire last round is another simple but effective color variation. This creates a frame for each block within the set and also creates a secondary octagonal pattern in the quilt.

Spirals of color radiating out from the center give the Pineapple an entirely different look, similar to a Snail's Trail design. Also try rotating the blocks in this setting.

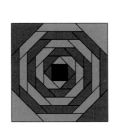 

Experiment with asymmetrical placement of color. Alternate fabrics along some sets of strips, but keep the fabrics the same along others. Rotate the block as you combine it in your quilt design. This setting creates a framed "flower."

The same block rotated in a different way results in a design that draws the eye out to the corners instead of into the center.

Tip

If you have a limited amount of fabric, use color photocopies of it to make a mock-up.

Changing the color of one corner expands the options even further. This design unifies the Pineapple strips in a block foursome and creates a focal point where the blocks come together.

A House Portrait
to Quilt

To capture the nostalgic image of your childhood home, your grandmother's house, or that quaint Victorian you've always admired, consider making a house portrait from fabric! Building a house in fabric is easier than you'd think; you just follow a full-scale design you create from a photo. No matter what your drawing skills, the instructions in this chapter from fiber artist Claudia McGill will show you how to create a pattern for a special house as seen from any angle. Your unique quilt is sure to cause viewers to stop and admire your "home sweet home" in fabric.

Getting Ready

Take several photos of the house you want to translate into fabric. A straight-on view will give you every detail of the front of your house and offer a flatter, more simplistic look, reminiscent of folk art. An angled view will give the finished fabric house a sense of dimension. Snap a few shots from various angles so you can assess all the candidates and choose your favorite view. You might want to have the "winning" photo enlarged to a 5 × 7 (or larger) format to make it easier to see and measure the details of the house.

Buy the largest sheets of ¼-inch graph paper you can find, or tape smaller sheets together to make one as large as your desired finished quilt.

The instructions here show how to do a fairly straightforward house—some details, but not too fussy—from two different angles. No matter what the style of *your* house, you'll be able to use these techniques to replicate it on paper, and then in fabric.

What You'll Need

Photo of the house

Large sheets of ¼" graph paper

Sharp pencil

Eraser

Notepad

Clear acrylic rulers:

   4" × 4" with ⅛" grid

   3" × 18"

Calculator

Fine-point permanent marker

Optional:

   Construction paper

   Paper scissors

Drafting a Straight-On View

Decide how big you want the finished size of the house to be. Allocating 3 to 5 inches per story (count the roof as one story) makes the house big enough to include most details. To create a full-scale drawing from your photo, begin with some simple math. First, measure the height of the house in your photo. **Divide the desired finished height by the photo height, and you have your enlargement factor.** For example, divide a 10½-inch finished house by a 1⅞-inch photo house, and the enlargement factor equals 5.6; round this number up to 6 to make the math easier.

Tip

When you simplify by rounding an uneven enlargement factor up or down, you end up with a slightly larger or smaller finished-size house.

101

2

Measure the bottom line, or baseline, of the house in your photo. Multiply this number by the enlargement factor you determined in Step 1 and draw the scaled-up baseline along a horizontal line at the bottom of the graph paper. (Make sure you have room to draw the rest of the house and landscaping around it.) Using this line as your reference point, **measure, multiply, and draw in the other lines that outline the house.** Afterward, draw any other major horizontal and vertical dividing lines: main roof lines, porch, gables, walls, and so on.

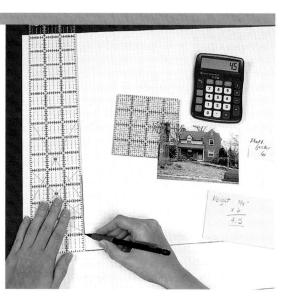

3

Tip

At this stage, concentrate on drafting the main roofline, and don't worry about any details such as dormers or chimneys.

To draw the angled right and left sides of the roof, use "triangulation." Place a small square ruler on the photo with the edges aligned with the roofline and the side of the house. **Measure in from the corner of the ruler to the corner of the roof** (here, ⅛ inch, where the pencil is pointing) and down, where the roof meets the side. Scale up these measurements and use a larger ruler on your drafted house to measure and mark the corresponding points. **Connect these points.** Repeat on the other side of the house.

4

Tip

Extend the angled lines of the dormer a little past the vertical "wall" lines for a more realistic look.

To create the large pointed dormer roof, draw an X connecting the corners of the vertical lines of the gable you drew in Step 2. Measure the photo to determine the distance between the point of the gable and the bottom of this rectangular area. Use your enlargement factor to scale up, measure, **and mark this point on your drawing. Align the ruler vertically with the intersection in the center of the X. Draw lines to connect the point of the gable with the top corners of the rectangle.** Erase the X.

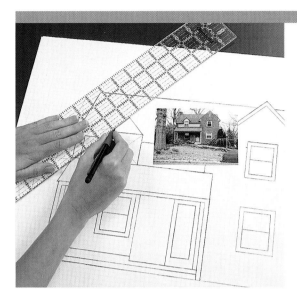

Taking measurements from your photo and reference points from the main lines of the house, draw the windows and doors. Draw the vertical lines first, then the horizontal ones. Begin with the outline of the trim, then delineate the glass area inside. If any windows or doors are partially obscured in the photo, draw the portion that you can see, and refer to photos taken from other angles to fill in the gaps. **For additional dormers or gables, use the technique described in Step 4 on the opposite page.**

Working in the same way, add details such as porches, chimneys, shutters, window boxes, or divisions between different construction materials. In this straight-on view, most of the features of your house will appear as simple, rectangular shapes. However **some, such as the chimney and the porch support, are at a slight angle to the viewer.** Keep alert for these small differences in perspective and use the method of triangulation described in Step 3 to draft them **so they look natural in the finished pattern,** just as in the photo.

Tip

If you've faithfully measured and drawn a feature and it just does not look right to you, adjust it to your liking.

Drafting an Angled View

In an angled view, none of your house's features are drawn as rectangles. The vertical lines in your photo will still be vertical in your drawing, but the horizontal lines all "angle off" toward an imaginary point in the distance. Use triangulation (see Step 3 on page 102) to plot each feature.

Measure the vertical line at the corner of the house that appears closest to you. Scale it up using the enlargement factor (see Steps 1 and 2 on pages 101–102) and draw it on graph paper. Make sure you have enough room to draw the rest of the house around it.

Tip

When drafting an angled view, use the lines on your graph paper as guides for the vertical lines only.

A HOUSE PORTRAIT TO QUILT

2

Next, draft the sloping line at the top of the front face of the house (outlined in red), using triangulation to obtain the correct angle. **Place the small square ruler on the photo so you can measure in two directions: over from the top of the closest corner (the top of the line you have just drawn) and down to the top point of the wall on the opposite side of the front of the house.** Use your enlargement factor to scale these measurements up, then **measure over and down on your drawing and mark this point.**

3

On the photo, measure from the point you just marked to the ground-level corner of the house. (If you cannot clearly see the ground line of the house in the photo, use the lines of the foundation or basement windows as a guide.) **Scale this measurement up and draw the line, which is the opposite side of the front of the house.** Connect the tops of these lines, then the bottoms, and you will have completed the front side of the house.

Repeat Steps 2 and 3 to draw in the side of the house visible in your photo.

4

To draft the gabled roofline, draw an X connecting the corners of the side of the house below it. Measure the photo to determine the distance between the peak of the gable and the bottom of the rectangle. Use your enlargement factor to scale up this measurement, and **mark this point on your drawing, with the ruler placed vertically through the intersection of the X. Draw lines to connect the point of the gable with the top corners of the house.** Erase the X.

To draft the roof, use triangulation (see Step 3 on page 102) to determine the point where the top of the roofline ends (near the chimney, in our photo). **Measure, scale up, and mark this point,** then draw a line connecting it to the top of the gable for the main roofline. Also draw a line connecting this new point with the top corner of the front of the house to create the slope of the roof.

To draw windows and doors, use triangulation in reference to the main lines of the house to measure and plot them. Start with the features that are closest to the first line you drew. Measure and draft the vertical lines first, then the horizontal ones.

Draw the porch, including any steps, and the chimney. Add any other prominent details, such as window mullions, shutters, and other trim.

Tip

To simplify your drawing, don't bother drafting any photo details that will scale up to less than ¼" in size.

Finishing Your House Portrait

The Final Design

Go over the lines of the house with a permanent black marker, and then erase any stray pencil lines. Use a pencil to sketch in the outlines of trees, shrubs, and any other decorative features. **Try out various landscaping options using construction paper cutouts that you can audition in different locations.**

Use your completed drawing to create freezer-paper pattern pieces for the various parts of the house, as well as the landscaping. See pages 106–113 for tips on cutting, piecing, and appliqué techniques.

Tip

Fusible appliqué is a fun, easy way to translate your house portrait to fabric.

A HOUSE PORTRAIT TO QUILT

Tips for Cutting, Piecing & Appliqué

Traditional drafting techniques result in exact, finished-size patterns. Here is a quick review of some cutting, piecing, and appliqué techniques that you'll need when you move beyond your drafted pattern or design and start to work in fabric.

Cutting & Piecing

Your drafted pattern is your guide for cutting out the patches that make up your block, no matter which piecing method you choose. For rotary cutting, your pattern will serve as a measuring guide. To work with templates, either traditional plastic or freezer paper, you'll use your pattern to make the templates. For foundation piecing, you'll trace or copy the pattern onto your foundation material.

Rotary Cutting

For straight-line geometric shapes that are easily measured, you can rely on rotary cutting with a clear acrylic ruler to cut your patches. This method applies best to squares, rectangles, and half- and quarter-square triangles. Note that many other shapes can be easily rotary cut; refer to your favorite rotary cutting reference book for instructions.

Cutting squares and rectangles. Measure the finished (drawn) height of a square or rectangle on your pattern. Add ½ inch for seam allowances, and cut a strip to that larger width. For squares, cut the strip into segments equal to its width. For rectangles, measure the length of the patch, add ½ inch for seam allowances, and cut the strip into segments of that measurement.

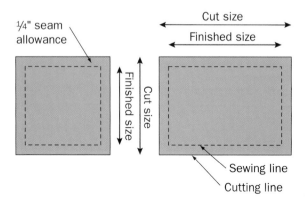

Cutting half-square triangles. A half-square triangle is made by cutting a square in half diagonally. Its longer side is a bias (stretchy) edge, while its two shorter sides have edges cut along the straight, stable grain. Measure your drawing to determine the finished length of either short side of the triangle. Add ⅞ inch for seam allowances, and cut a fabric square with that larger measurement. Cut the square in half diagonally once to yield two identical half-square triangles.

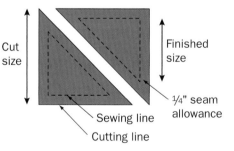

Cutting quarter-square triangles. A quarter-square triangle is made by cutting a square in half diagonally in both directions to form four triangles. Its two shorter sides are bias (stretchy) edges, while its longer side has an edge cut along the more stable straight grain. Measure your drawing to find the finished length of the longer side of the triangle. Add 1¼ inches for seam allowances, and cut a fabric square with that larger measurement. Cut the square in half diagonally in both directions to yield four quarter-square triangles.

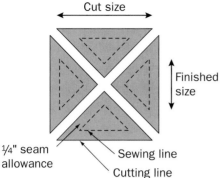

Cut size

Finished size

¼" seam allowance

Sewing line

Cutting line

Plastic Templates

Many quilters like to work with finished-size templates because they can easily mark and sew along the stitching line. Some patterns also lend themselves more readily to templates, such as blocks with curves; very intricate blocks; blocks with patch sizes that aren't easily measured with a ruler; and blocks with shapes other than squares, rectangles, and triangles. Follow these steps to make accurate templates for hand or machine piecing.

1. Lay translucent template plastic over your drawn pattern, making sure it completely covers the patch you want to trace. *For hand piecing:* Use a fine-point permanent marker to trace the outline of the patch onto your template plastic (use a ruler to trace straight lines). *For machine piecing:* Use a clear acrylic ruler and a fine-point permanent marker to draw ¼ inch outside the lines of the patch (this is your cutting line). If desired, you can also draw dashed sewing lines by tracing around the outline of the patch.

2. Cut out your template with sharp utility scissors or a sharp craft knife (use a rotary ruler to cut straight lines safely and accurately). Adhere sandpaper dots or double-stick tape to the underside of the template to keep it from slipping when placed on the fabric. To prevent the fabric from shifting and to ensure crisp points, place your fabric on a piece of fine-grain sandpaper when you trace around your shapes. Trace around the template onto the wrong side of your fabric. *For hand piecing:* Cut out the patch, leaving at least ¼ inch of extra fabric outside the drawn sewing line for seam allowances. *For machine piecing:* Cut out the patch along the drawn line with scissors or a rotary cutter and ruler.

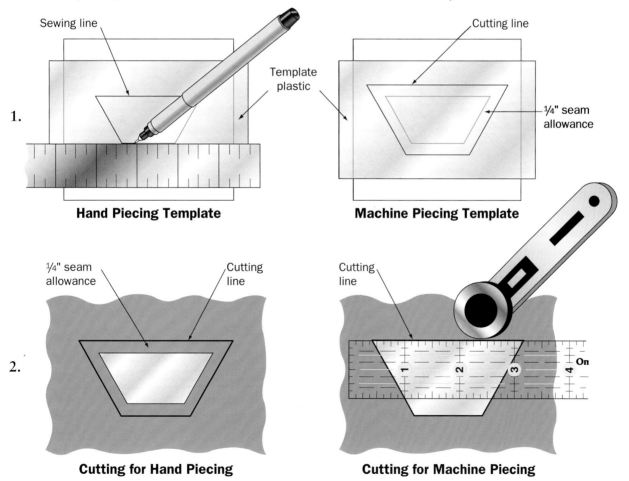

1. Sewing line

Template plastic

Hand Piecing Template

Cutting line

¼" seam allowance

Machine Piecing Template

2. ¼" seam allowance

Cutting line

Cutting for Hand Piecing

Cutting line

Cutting for Machine Piecing

To cut mirror-image or reversed pieces, lay two pieces of fabric right sides together, then mark and cut both layers at the same time.

Freezer Paper Templates

Freezer paper, available at most grocery stores, also makes excellent template material. It's a great choice when you have shapes with bias edges or sharp, spiky points, as in a Mariner's Compass or Blazing Star. Leaving the freezer paper pressed to the fabric as you sew the patches together helps to stabilize bias edges and keeps them from stretching out of shape.

1. Trace the entire block onto the dull, non-waxy side of the freezer paper, then cut it apart along the lines to make a separate template for each patch in the quilt. Label each template so you know its position in relation to the other patches.

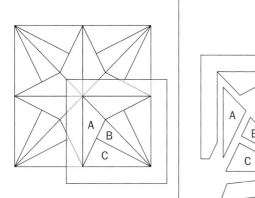

2. Use a dry iron to press the waxy (shiny) side of the freezer paper onto the wrong side of the fabric. Then either eyeball and cut with scissors or use a rotary ruler and cutter to cut out the patch ¼ inch outside the freezer paper template.

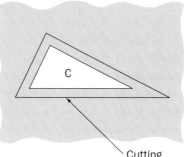

Cutting line

3. When assembling your block, use the edges of the freezer paper to position and pin the patches together. Then sew along the edge of the freezer paper template.

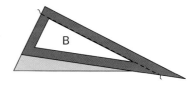

Foundations

Stitching on foundations stabilizes patches, prevents bias edges from stretching, and produces incredibly accurate points, seam joins, and small shapes. For many blocks, foundation piecing is the way to go. Blocks that are pieced "in the round," such as Log Cabin and Pineapple blocks, are particularly well-suited to foundation piecing. Other good candidates are blocks that are pieced diagonally across the block, like Roman Stripes, or from one side to the other, like Flying Geese. Tracing paper, freezer paper, and temporary interfacing are all good choices for foundation materials. Your quilt shop also carries specialty papers made specifically for foundation piecing.

1. Trace your pattern onto a suitable foundation material.

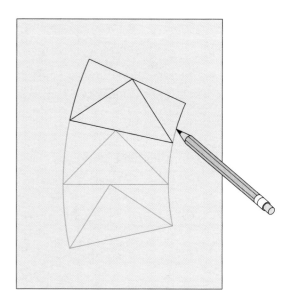

2. Cut oversize pieces of fabric for each patch you will sew. Most foundation-pieced patterns begin either in the middle (for circular patterns such as Pineapple blocks) or move from one side to the other (as in a

Flying Geese section). Place the fabric for the first patch wrong side down on the unmarked side of the foundation. Hold the foundation up to the light to see that the fabric completely covers the patch area, with at least ¼ inch overlap for seam allowances. Pin the fabric in place.

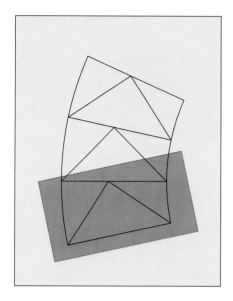

4. Set your machine to sew a short stitch, about 16 stitches per inch (generally, 12 stitches per inch is the norm for piecing). Turn the foundation over so the marked side is facing up, and sew along the drawn seam line between the first two patches, extending the stitching about ⅛ inch beyond the seam line at each end.

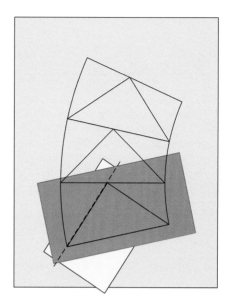

3. Place the fabric for the second patch on top of the first patch with right sides together, positioning it so that when it is sewn in place and flipped open it will cover its intended patch area. (You may find it helpful to pin it along the stitching line, flip it open, and hold it up to the light to make sure it is positioned correctly.) When you have it positioned correctly, check your pin placement to make sure it won't interfere as you sew the seam.

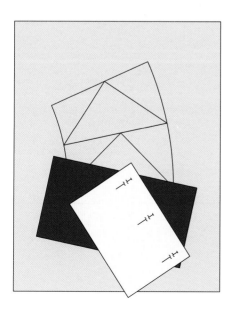

5. Remove the foundation from the machine, and clip the threads at each end of the seam line close to the foundation. Turn the foundation over to the fabric side, fold the foundation along the seam you just stitched, and trim the seam allowance to a scant ¼ inch. Flip open the second fabric patch and use a hot, dry iron to press it in place. Or you can gently but firmly finger-press the patch open with your fingertips.

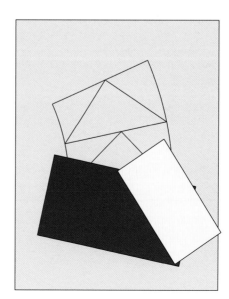

6. Continue to add patches in this manner until your block or strip is complete. Trim all seam allowances along the outer edges of the block to ¼ inch, using a rotary ruler and cutter for straight edges and scissors for curves.

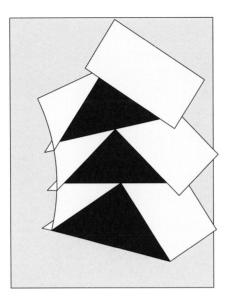

Leave the foundation in place until the block or section is sewn into your quilt, then carefully rip the paper away at each sewn seam.

Sewing Accurately

If you've taken the time to draft your own pattern, you'll want to make sure that you sew it accurately. The biggest obstacle to this can be seam allowances that do not measure a precise, consistent ¼ inch. Your presser foot or machine markings do not guarantee that you are sewing accurately. In fact, your fabrics, thread, and machine needle can all affect the width of your seam allowance. Start each new project with this simple test to ensure that your sewing is as accurate as possible.

1. Cut two squares from your fabrics, each exactly 2 inches. Sew them together along one side. Remove them from your machine and measure the seam allowance. Including the thread, it should measure exactly ¼ inch.

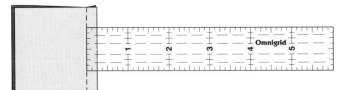

2. Open out the squares and press the seam allowances to one side. Now measure each square; they should measure exactly 1¾ inches wide each. If these measurements are not accurate, adjust your stitching and repeat the test. Once you achieve perfect seams, mark your machine bed with masking tape so you have an exact guide as you sew.

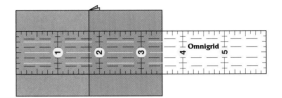

Sewing Curves

Many of the patterns shown in this book, and the patterns you may create yourself, have curves. Don't talk yourself out of a particular quilt block just because it has curved seams! With a little practice, you can sew curved seams that lie just as flat as straight ones. Just follow the steps below.

1. Place your two patches with right sides together and the patch with the concave (inner) curve on top. Match and pin the midpoints of the curves. (Most patterns will have you mark the midpoint for sewing.)

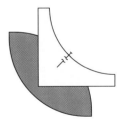

2. If your concave patch has sharp curves, you'll need to clip them to make sewing your curve easier. Use a small pair of scissors to clip into the seam allowance along the concave (inner) curve, stopping two or three threads before the sewing line.

3. Pin the ends of the patches together, aligning the cut edges. Then pin again between the center and the ends. Add additional pins if your curve is a long one.

4. Set your machine to sew a shorter stitch length than usual, about 16 stitches per inch. Sew slowly along the seam line, stopping and removing pins just before the needle comes to them. You will need to pivot slightly between stitches to maintain the shape of the curve.

5. Press the seam allowances toward the convex piece so the unit lays flat.

Set-In Seams

Many patterns, once drafted, cannot be pieced entirely with straight seams. Sometimes you'll find that your pattern includes pieces that nest together along an angle, and when that happens, you'll need to set in the piece that fits into the angle. Sometimes, you may even need to sew an entire sequence of set-in seams to get the results you want. Examples of these patterns can be best seen in "Stars for Stellar Quilts" on page 58 and "Wonderful One Patch Quilts" on page 24.

The key to sewing set-in seams is to sew only from seam allowance to seam allowance, and never to stitch into or across seam allowances. The directions here are for sewing

together three diamonds, as for a Tumbling Blocks pattern, but you'll set in other seams using the same basic method.

1. Mark the seam line intersections on the wrong sides of all your patches. You can use a small ruler to measure in ¼ inch from the edges, and mark a dot at each angle. Place two adjacent pieces with right sides together and pin exactly through the dots so you know that the seam you will sew starts and ends exactly at the right place.

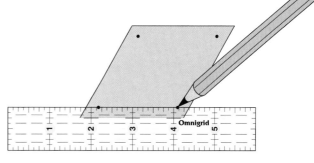

2. Sew the seam from marked dot to marked dot, backstitching at the beginning and the end. This will secure your line of stitching and still leave the seam allowances free.

3. Open out the sewn patches, and pin the third one to one side of the pair. Sew the seam as before. Then pin the last seam, again sewing from dot to dot so the seam allowances remain free and unsewn. Press carefully, so as not to stretch the seams out of shape.

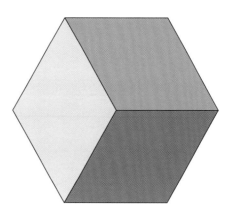

Appliqué

There are many methods of appliqué to choose from. Here are brief directions for a few popular methods; refer to your favorite appliqué reference book for more details. Choose the technique that will give you the look and feel you want and that matches your preference for hand or machine work, time limitations, and available materials. For example, traditional edge-turn appliqué will give you soft edges and dimension, whereas satin-stitching around fused appliqués will add the design element of a contrasting outline and a crisp, firm result.

Turned-Edge Appliqué

1. Make finished-size templates for all the shapes you need to appliqué. Use your fabric marking tool to trace the shape onto the right side of the fabric, then cut it out, adding scant ¼-inch seam allowances as you cut.

2. Baste the seam allowance edges in place with a running stitch and contrasting color thread, turning the seam allowance to the wrong side as you go. Make sure your marked line is hidden at the back of the shape. Finger-press lightly if desired.

3. If you have deep points or tight curves, use small, sharp scissors to clip into the seam allowance to within a thread or two of the drawn line, so the edges of the shape lie flat and you avoid the bulk of a pleat.

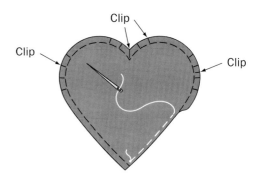

4. Position your appliqué shape on the background as desired, and pin it into place. Sew the shape onto the background, using a blind stitch in a matching thread color. Make your stitches as small as possible, placing them approximately ⅛ inch apart around the entire shape.

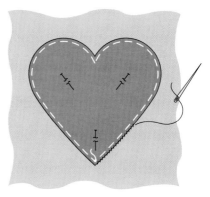

Machine Appliqué

For a quicker method of edge-turn appliqué, try this freezer-paper method of machine appliqué. Use nylon thread instead of regular sewing thread in your machine (clear for light fabrics, smoke for dark ones) for a nearly invisible stitch.

1. Trace the appliqué shape from your drafted pattern onto the dull, nonwaxy side of a piece of freezer paper. Cut it out on the drawn line. Pin the shape to the wrong side of your fabric, with the shiny side facing up. Cut out the shape, leaving a scant ¼-inch seam allowance around the entire shape. Clip along the curves. Use the tip of a hot, dry iron to press the seam allowance over the edge of the paper and down onto the freezer paper.

Clip

2. Pin the appliqué in place on the background fabric. Set your machine to sew a blind-hem stitch with a very short and narrow stitch length and width. (If your machine doesn't have a blind-hem stitch, substitute a narrow zigzag stitch.) Thread your machine with nylon monofilament thread, and fill your bobbin with a sewing thread that matches the color of your background. Sew the shape to the background, taking as tiny a bite as possible out of the edge of the appliqué shape.

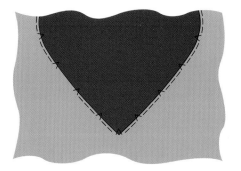

3. Stop stitching about ¾ inch before the place you started. Use tweezers to grasp and gently tug the freezer paper out from between the appliqué and the background, then complete the stitching.

Fusible Appliqué

The quickest method of appliqué is to fuse your shapes into place and then anchor them onto the background with machine stitching.

1. Trace the desired shapes onto the paper backing of a piece of fusible web. Note that your finished design will be a mirror image of what you trace onto the paper, so reverse your design before you trace it, if necessary. Cut out the shape slightly beyond the marked outlines, and follow the manufacturer's instructions to fuse the paper-backed web onto the wrong side of your fabric.

2. Cut out the fabric shape, exactly following the edges of the drawn design. Remove the paper and place the fabric shape onto your background fabric as desired. Fuse it in place, following the manufacturer's directions. Fused appliqués may eventually lift away from the background, so stitch along their edges to secure them permanently. Use a machine blindstitch and matching thread (or clear monofilament) for a nearly invisible finish. Or, for embellishment, use decorative machine stitches and a contrasting-color thread to machine appliqué your motif.

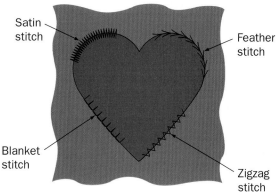

Satin stitch

Feather stitch

Blanket stitch

Zigzag stitch

Handy
Reference Charts

Equivalency Charts

Decimal & Fraction Equivalents

Fractions	Decimals
1/16	0.0625
1/8	0.125
3/16	0.1875
1/4	0.25
5/16	0.3125
3/8	0.375
7/16	0.4375
1/2	0.5
9/16	0.5625
5/8	0.625
11/16	0.6875
3/4	0.75
13/16	0.8125
7/8	0.875
15/16	0.9375

Yardage & Inches Equivalents

Note: To convert for dimensions larger than 1 yard, add the fraction to the larger yardage number.

Yards	Inches
1/8	4½
1/4	9
1/3	12
3/8	13½
1/2	18
5/8	22½
2/3	24
3/4	27
7/8	31½
1	36
2	72
3	108
4	144
5	180
6	216
7	252
8	288

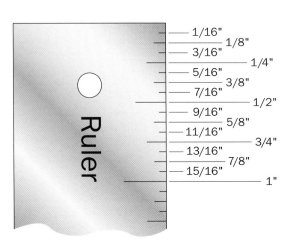

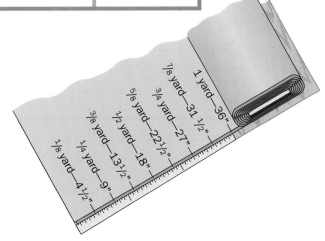

Metric Conversion Charts

Yards to Meters

yards	meters	yards	meters	yards	meters	yards	meters	yards	meters
⅛	0.11	2⅛	1.94	4⅛	3.77	6⅛	5.60	8⅛	7.43
¼	0.23	2¼	2.06	4¼	3.89	6¼	5.72	8¼	7.54
⅜	0.34	2⅜	2.17	4⅜	4.00	6⅜	5.83	8⅜	7.66
½	0.46	2½	2.29	4½	4.11	6½	5.94	8½	7.77
⅝	0.57	2⅝	2.40	4⅝	4.23	6⅝	6.06	8⅝	7.89
¾	0.69	2¾	2.51	4¾	4.34	6¾	6.17	8¾	8.00
⅞	0.80	2⅞	2.63	4⅞	4.46	6⅞	6.29	8⅞	8.12
1	0.91	3	2.74	5	4.57	7	6.40	9	8.23
1⅛	1.03	3⅛	2.86	5⅛	4.69	7⅛	6.52	9⅛	8.34
1¼	1.14	3¼	2.97	5¼	4.80	7¼	6.63	9¼	8.46
1⅜	1.26	3⅜	3.09	5⅜	4.91	7⅜	6.74	9⅜	8.57
1½	1.37	3½	3.20	5½	5.03	7½	6.86	9½	8.69
1⅝	1.49	3⅝	3.31	5⅝	5.14	7⅝	6.97	9⅝	8.80
1¾	1.60	3¾	3.43	5¾	5.26	7¾	7.09	9¾	8.921
1⅞	1.71	3⅞	3.54	5⅞	5.37	7⅞	7.20	9⅞	9.03
2	1.83	4	3.66	6	5.49	8	7.32	10	9.14

Inches to Millimeters and Centimeters

mm = millimeters; cm = centimeters

inches	mm	cm	inches	cm	inches	cm
⅛	3	0.3	9	22.9	30	76.2
¼	6	0.6	10	25.4	31	78.7
⅜	10	1.0	11	27.9	32	81.3
½	13	1.3	12	30.5	33	83.8
⅝	16	1.6	13	33.0	34	86.4
¾	19	1.9	14	35.6	35	88.9
⅞	22	2.2	15	38.1	36	91.4
1	25	2.5	16	40.6	37	94.0
1¼	32	3.2	17	43.2	38	96.5
1½	38	3.8	18	45.7	39	99.1
1¾	44	4.4	19	48.3	40	101.6
2	51	5.1	20	50.8	41	104.1
2½	64	6.4	21	53.3	42	106.7
3	76	7.6	22	55.9	43	109.2
3½	89	8.9	23	58.4	44	111.8
4	102	10.2	24	61.0	45	114.3
4½	114	11.4	25	63.5	46	116.8
5	127	12.7	26	66.0	47	119.4
6	152	15.2	27	68.6	48	121.9
7	178	17.8	28	71.1	49	124.5
8	203	20.3	29	73.7	50	127.0

HANDY REFERENCE CHARTS

Bed & Quilt Sizes (in Inches)

Bed Size	Mattress Size	Batting Size	Final Quilt Size*
Crib	23 × 46	45 × 60	45 × 60, maximum
Twin	39 × 75	72 × 90	59 × 85
Double/Full	54 × 75	81 × 96	74 × 85
Queen	60 × 80	90 × 108	80 × 90
King	76 × 80	120 × 120	96 × 90

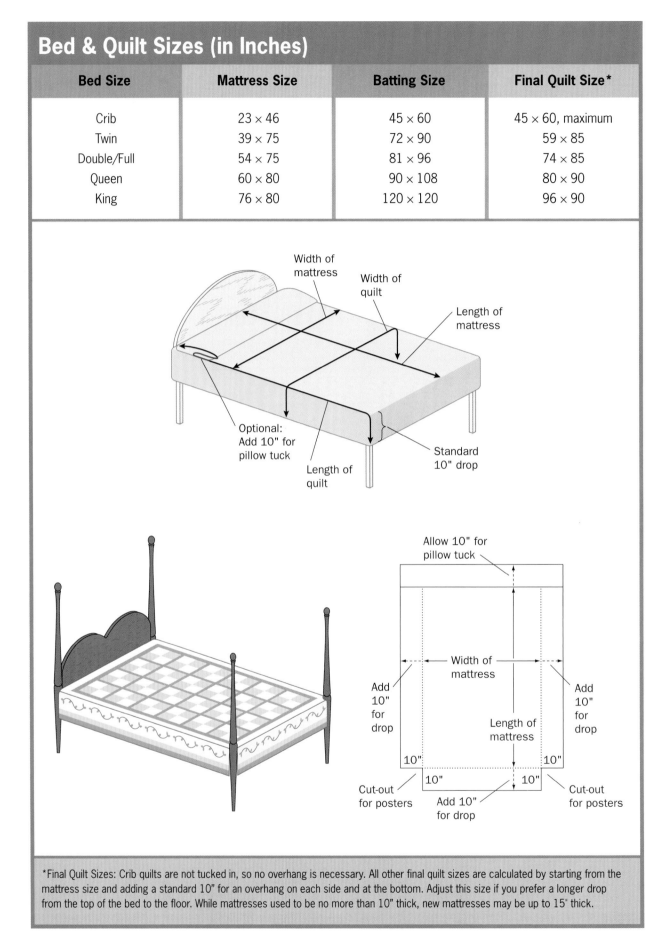

*Final Quilt Sizes: Crib quilts are not tucked in, so no overhang is necessary. All other final quilt sizes are calculated by starting from the mattress size and adding a standard 10" for an overhang on each side and at the bottom. Adjust this size if you prefer a longer drop from the top of the bed to the floor. While mattresses used to be no more than 10" thick, new mattresses may be up to 15" thick.

Measurements for On-Point Quilts (All Measurements in Inches)

Block Size (finished)	Diagonal Measurement of Finished Block	Side Setting Triangle Cut a square this size; cut diagonally twice into 4 triangles.	Corner Triangle Cut a square this size; cut diagonally once into 2 triangles.
3	4¼	5½	3
4	5⅝	7	3¾
5	7⅛	8⅜	4½
6	8½	9¾	5⅛
7	9⅞	11¼	5⅞
8	11⅜	12⅝	6⅝
9	12¾	14	7¼
10	14⅛	15½	8
11	15½	16⅞	8¾
12	17	18¼	9⅜
13	18⅜	19¾	10⅛
14	19¾	21⅛	10⅞
15	21¼	22½	11½

Math formulas:
Diagonal measurement: finished size × 1.414 (round to nearest ⅛ inch) (10 × 1.414 = 14.14; round to 14⅛)
Side triangle: finished size × 1.414 + 1.25 inches; round up to nearest ⅛ inch. (10-inch block: 10 × 1.414 = 14.14 + 1.25 = 15.39 or 15½ inches)
Corner triangle: finished size ÷ 1.414 + .875 inch; round up to nearest ⅛ inch. (10-inch block: 10 ÷ 1.414 = 7.07 + .875 = 7.94 or 8 inches)

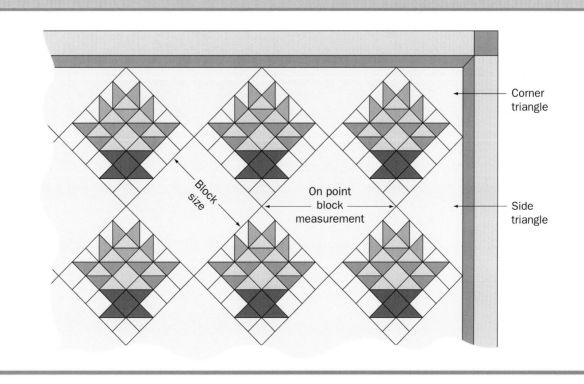

Corner triangle

Block size

On point block measurement

Side triangle

Reduction & Enlargement

To use this chart, locate the finished size of the block (as shown in your quilt pattern or drafting) along the vertical column at the far left. Determine what size you would like your block to be, and locate that measurement along the top horizontal row. The number where the column and row intersect is the percentage at which you set a photocopier. If the number is less than 100, you are making a reduction; if the number is more than 100, you are making an enlargement.

Block Size	Desired Block Size													
	2"	3"	4"	5"	6"	7"	8"	9"	10"	11"	12"	13"	14"	15"
2"	100.00	150.00	200.00	250.00	300.00	350.00	400.00	450.00	500.00	550.00	600.00	650.00	700.00	750.00
3"	66.67	100.00	133.33	166.67	200.00	233.33	266.67	300.00	333.33	366.67	400.00	433.33	466.67	500.00
4"	50.00	75.00	100.00	125.00	150.00	175.00	200.00	225.00	250.00	275.00	300.00	325.00	350.00	375.00
5"	40.00	60.00	80.00	100.00	120.00	140.00	160.00	180.00	200.00	220.00	240.00	260.00	280.00	300.00
6"	33.33	50.00	66.67	83.33	100.00	116.67	133.33	150.00	166.67	183.33	200.00	216.67	233.33	250.00
7"	28.57	42.86	57.14	71.43	85.71	100.00	114.29	128.57	142.86	157.14	171.43	185.71	200.00	214.29
8"	25.00	37.50	50.00	62.50	75.00	87.50	100.00	112.50	125.00	137.50	150.00	162.50	175.00	187.50
9"	22.22	33.33	44.44	55.56	66.67	77.78	88.89	100.00	111.11	122.22	133.33	144.44	155.56	166.67
10"	20.00	30.00	40.00	50.00	60.00	70.00	80.00	90.00	100.00	110.00	120.00	130.00	140.00	150.00
11"	18.18	27.27	36.36	45.45	54.55	63.64	72.73	81.82	90.91	100.00	109.09	118.18	127.27	136.36
12"	16.67	25.00	33.33	41.67	50.00	58.33	66.67	75.00	83.33	91.67	100.00	108.33	116.67	125.00
13"	15.38	23.08	30.77	38.46	46.15	53.85	61.54	69.23	76.92	84.62	92.31	100.00	107.69	115.38
14"	14.29	21.43	28.57	35.71	42.86	50.00	57.14	64.29	71.43	78.57	85.71	92.86	100.00	107.14
15"	13.33	20.00	26.67	33.33	40.00	46.67	53.33	60.00	66.67	73.33	80.00	86.67	93.33	100.00

Math Formula: Desired size ÷ Existing size = % enlarged or reduced (8 ÷ 9 = 88.89%; round up to 89%)

Calculating Yardages for Your Quilts

To figure out exactly how much of each fabric you will need, first count the quantity of each shape, both appliqué and pieced. Use the "Cutting Shapes" table below to determine the size strip you'll need for most common patchwork shapes. The diagram at right shows how to convert appliqué shapes and less-common patch shapes to squares or rectangles. Then, use the "Yardage Calculation" worksheet below to plug in your quantities, sizes, and fabrics. You'll end up with a shopping list of fabric yardages that you can take right to the fabric shop.

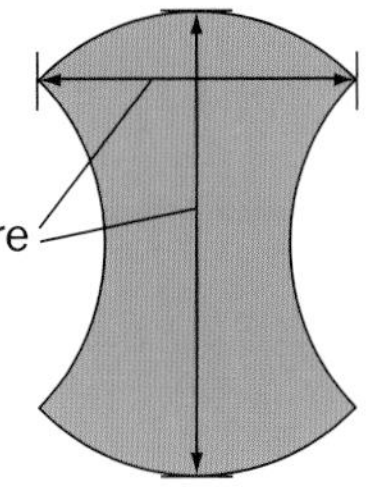

Measure here

Cutting Shapes

Shape		Strip Width	Cut Length
Squares		Finished height + ½"	Finished length + ½"
Rectangles		Finished height + ½"	Finished length + ½"
Half-square triangles		Finished length of short edge + ⅞"	Finished length of short edge + ⅞"
Quarter-square triangles		Finished length of long edge + 1¼"	Finished length of long edge + 1¼"
Equilateral triangles		Finished height + ¾"	Finished leg length + ⅞"

Yardage Calculation Worksheet

Column 1	Column 2	Column 3	Column 4	Column 5	Column 6	Column 7	Column 8
Fabric	Piece	No. of Pieces Needed	Dimensions (Cut size)	Pieces per Strip	No. of Strips Needed	Total Inches Needed	Total Yardage
				40 ÷ piece length*	Divide Column 3 by Column 5†	Multiply Column 6 by strip width	Divide Column 7 by 36" and add extra for "insurance"‡

*Round down to nearest whole number.
†Round up to nearest whole number.
‡Add at least one extra strip width in case of a cutting error.

Calculating Yardage for Binding

Yardage for Straight-Grain Binding

Cut width of binding (inches)	Yardage* needed if your binding length (in inches) is:				
	Up to 150	150–200	200–350	350–450	450–500
1	¼	¼	⅓	⅜	½
1½	¼	⅓	½	⅝	⅝
2	⅓	⅓	⅝	¾	⅞
2½	⅓	½	¾	1	1
3	⅜	½	⅞	1⅛	1¼
3½	½	⅝	1	1¼	1⅓
4	½	⅝	1⅛	1½	1½
4½	⅝	⅔	1¼	1⅝	1¾
5	⅝	¾	1⅓	1¾	1⅞
5½	⅔	⅞	1½	2	2⅛
6	¾	1	1⅝	2⅛	2¼

*Based on strips cut crosswise from 40"-wide prewashed fabric.

Yardage for Bias Binding

Cut width of binding (inches)	Yardage* needed if your binding length (in inches) is:		
	Up to 200	200–350	350–500
1	½	⅝	¾
1½	⅝	¾	⅞
2	⅝	⅞	1
2½	¾	⅞	1⅛
3	¾	1	1⅛
3½	⅞	1	1¼
4	⅞	1⅛	1⅜
4½	⅞	1⅛	1⅜
5	1	1¼	1½
5½	1	1¼	1½
6	1	1⅜	1⅝

*Based on strips cut on a 45-degree angle from 40"-wide prewashed fabric.

Drafting & Design
Glossary

A

Acute angle. An angle that measures less than 90 degrees. These "sharp" angles form a narrow point.

Arc. A segment or portion of a circle.

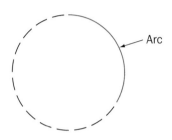

Arc

Asymmetry. The characteristic of a composition in which shapes, lines, colors, or values appear in an uneven distribution.

C

Compass. A tool with an adjustable span that allows you to draw perfect circles and arcs in the exact size you desire.

Concentric circles. Circles of different sizes that all have the same center point.

Cursor. On a computer, the small icon that moves on your screen as you move your mouse. In computer software, it is often an arrow or a pointing finger used to select options or tools, and it can change to represent the current tool.

D

Diameter. The distance from a point on the outer edge of a circle, through the center of the circle, to a point on the opposite edge. The diameter is exactly twice the radius.

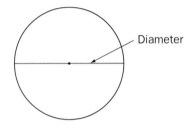

Diameter

Diamond. A shape with four equal sides and opposite angles that are equal.

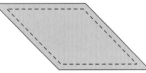

Drop-down menu. A list of options or actions on a computer that remains hidden until you act to display it. Usually, this is done by clicking on a command located at the top of the screen.

E

Equilateral triangle. A three-sided figure in which all three sides are of equal length and all three angles measure exactly 60 degrees.

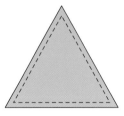

F

Flexible grid. A method of drafting that enables you to divide a square of any size into any amount of equal divisions.

Four-block set. Four identical blocks, arranged in an adjacent 2 by 2 grid. Secondary patterns frequently emerge when blocks are set together this way.

Freezer paper. Actually a kitchen product, freezer paper has a waxy coating on one side that sticks to fabric when pressed with an iron. This ability to temporarily adhere makes it useful as a template material.

G

Graph paper. Gridded paper that can be used to draft quilt blocks and design quilts. The most common graph paper has lines ¼ inch apart. Isometric graph paper has a preprinted grid of 60-degree triangles; it's helpful for planning

121

hexagon-based and 60-degree diamond designs.

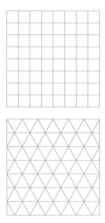

Grid-based block. A block that can be divided into an equal number of square units vertically and horizontally.

I

Isometric graph paper. *See* Graph paper.

L

Light box. A glass- or Plexiglas-topped box containing a bright light, ideal for tracing designs or patterns.

O

Obtuse angle. An angle that measures more than 90 degrees. These "wide" angles form a broad point.

Opaque projector. A machine that can project an opaque, flat image, such as a picture or photograph, onto a wall.

Overhead projector. A machine that can project transparency film that has been printed, photocopied, written, or drawn upon onto a wall.

P

Parallel lines. Lines that remain the same distance apart along their entire length and never intersect.

Perpendicular lines. Lines that intersect at a 90-degree angle.

Perspective. The representation of objects on a flat surface so that they appear three-dimensional, as they do to the eye in reality.

Proportional scale. A handy wheel-like tool that allows you to determine what percentage to enlarge or reduce a block or appliqué motif so that it fits properly in your quilt.

Protractor. A circular or semi-circular tool that enables you to measure and mark precise angles.

Q

Quarter-square triangle. A triangle obtained by cutting a square in half diagonally twice, resulting in four triangles with their longest edges along the straight grain.

R

Radius. The distance from the center of a circle to any point on the outer edge of the circle. The radius is exactly one-half the diameter.

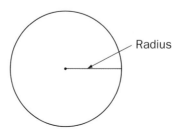

Radius

S

Scaling up. Altering the drawn size of an object to a larger size by using a multiplication factor to increase proportionately all dimensions of the object.

Slide projector. A projector that displays 2-inch cardboard- or plastic-mounted transparencies onto a wall or screen.

Symmetry. The characteristic of a composition when shapes, lines, colors, and values are repeated exactly the same from side to side or top to bottom.

T

Template. A piece of plastic or other rigid material cut in the shape of an appliqué, piecing, or quilting shape; it's used as a tracing guide to transfer the shape onto fabric.

Tool bar. A group of buttons or boxes on a computer screen that provide shortcuts for commands or actions.

Trapezoid. A four-sided figure in which two opposite sides are parallel, but the remaining two sides are not.

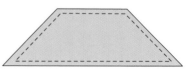

Y

Yardstick compass. A two-piece, clip-on notion designed to adapt a standard yardstick or ruler to draw a circle or arc larger than the span of a typical compass.

Charlotte Warr Andersen has been a quilter for 27 years and has focused for the last 17 years on making one-of-a-kind pictorial quilts using both piecing and appliqué. Her specialty is making realistic portraits in fabric; her quilt, NAIAD, was chosen as one of the Hundred Best Quilts of the Twentieth Century. She is the author of two books, *Faces & Places—Images in Appliqué* and *Focus on Features—Life-Like Portrayals in Appliqué.* As a quilting instructor, Charlotte travels to national and international venues.

Karen Kay Buckley lives in Carlisle, Pennsylvania, with her husband, Joe; their cat, Sassy; and their dogs, Sasha and Tillie. Karen graduated from Lock Haven University with a degree in education. She has been quilting for 18 years and teaching quilting for 13 years. She has over 250 quilts to her credit, and they have won numerous national and regional awards, including six Best of Show awards. Her quilts have graced the covers of many magazines. She has four books published with AQS.

Elsie M. Campbell began exhibiting quilts on the national level in 1992 and has won such prestigious awards as First Place Traditional Pieced at the International Quilt Festival in Houston and Best of Show at Quilt America! in Indianapolis. She is a writer and editor for Chitra Publications, publishers of *Miniature Quilts, Quilting Today,* and *Traditional Quiltworks* magazines. She works from her home in Dodge City, Kansas, and travels throughout the United States teaching her quiltmaking techniques.

Karen Eckmeier has been designing her own quilts since 1996. Her quilts have won numerous awards and have appeared in several quilting magazines. Currently Karen has been concentrating on painting her own fabrics and using them in a series of fabric collages. She does commission work and offers workshops on her Topstitch Piecing technique.

Gloria Hansen is an award-winning quiltmaker who, since 1990, has been using Macintosh computers to help design quilts. Gloria is the author of *Free Stuff for Traveling Quilters on the Internet,* the co-author of *The Quilter's Computer Companion,* and the author or co-author of 12 other quilt- or computer-related books. She has written for leading craft, quilting, and computer publications, has self-published patterns, and her quilts have been featured in numerous magazine articles and books, and on television. Gloria lives in East Windsor Township, New Jersey, where she also works as a Web site designer and consultant. She invites you to visit her at www.gloriahansen.com.

Dixie Haywood is the author of six books, four written with Jane Hall. Both Jane and Dixie have long been fascinated by the infinite possibilities of the pieced Pineapple. Dixie has been quilting continuously since the late 1960s and has been a teacher, lecturer, and judge on the national scene since the publication of her first book in 1977. She lives in Pensacola, Florida, where, in addition to quiltmaking, she enjoys swimming, cooking, and gardening.

Claudia McGill is an artist whose philosophy is "Give it a try and see what happens!" A former banker, her initial interest in fiber art was sparked by the need to do something with the fabric scraps from 30 windows' worth of curtains. Her award-winning work has appeared in numerous art shows and invitational exhibitions in the mid-Atlantic region. As an outgrowth of her fiber art, she has recently begun working and exhibiting in paper collage as well, with the happy result of gaining some new perspectives on fabric art.

Darra Duffy Williamson has been quilting for 20 years, and will be forever grateful to her first quilting teacher, who taught pattern drafting from day one. Since stitching that first quilt, Darra has made over 150 more; won awards at local, regional, and national shows; taught quilting classes all over the United States, in Europe, and on various quilting cruises; written, edited, or contributed to numerous quilting books and periodicals; and was honored as 1989 Quilt Teacher of the Year. Darra recently moved to the San Francisco Bay area, where she is editor-in-chief for C & T Publishing.

Joen Wolfrom is a quiltmaker, textile artist, author, lecturer, and instructor. She has taught and lectured in the quilting field both nationally and internationally since 1984. Additionally, she is invited to jury, judge, and curate quilt and textile art shows and exhibitions. Her best-selling books include *Color Play, The Visual Dance, Make Any Block Any Size, Patchwork Persuasion, The Magical Effects of Color,* and *Landscapes & Illusions.* Her love of color and nature and her inquisitive, creative character allow her to be innovative in both traditional and nontraditional quilting. Joen lives on Fox Island, a small island in western Washington.

Acknowledgments

We gratefully thank the many quilt designers who have generously contributed to this book.

Charlotte Warr Andersen, Sly Embrace, 2001, on page 30

Karen Kay Buckley, Friends Forever, 1996, with Barbara Schenck, Helen Sheibley, Lytle Markham, and Carmen Eiserman, and quilted by Dorothy Best, on page 80 and detail on the cover; Mariner's Compass, 1992, on page 85 and on the opposite page

Shelly Burge, Evening Star on the Farm, 1997, on page 58

Elsie M. Campbell, One Patch Times Four, 2001, on page 24 (fabrics provided by Primrose Gradations; see "Resources" on page 126)

Mary Jane Cook, Sunset-at-Sea, 2000, on pages 4–5

Ida May Davis, My Millennium, 2000, on page 10, as inspired by Irish Eyes by Irma Gail Hatcher, from her book *Hot Fudge Sundae & Irish Eyes, Plus 10 Secrets of Quilt Design*, 1994 (see "Resources" on page 126)

Karen Eckmeier, Comma Chameleon, 2001, on page 36 and detail on page 40; Willow, 2000, on page 42

Caryl Bryer Fallert, Migration #9, 2001, on page 86

Brooke Flynn, Sunset Wheel of Mystery, 2001, on pages 2–3, 64, and 71 (on loan from the David Small Invitational 2001)

Patricia Gabriel, Victorian Valentine, 1992, on page 18

Gloria Hansen, Breaking Free, 1994, on page 48

Dixie Haywood, Memories, 1988, on page 92 and detail on page 96

Claudia McGill, Along Orleans Way and On Lindley Road, both 2001, on page 100

Kathy Voth, Triple Chain with Star, 2000, on page 74 and detail on page 78 (courtesy of Haden Nickell)

Thanks to the following people who made samples: Elsie M. Campbell, Sarah Sacks Dunn, Karen Eckmeier, Eleanor Levie, and Claudia McGill.

The Wedding Ring quilt on page 14, circa 1930, is courtesy of Eleanor Levie.
Many of the photographs in this book were taken at Ethan Allen Home Interiors, Allentown, Pennsylvania.

Beaver Paper & Packaging
1605 Indian Brook Way
Building 300
Atlanta, GA 30093-2663
Phone: (800) 768-2700
Fax: (888) 768-2700
Web site:
www.beaverpaper.com
Alphanumeric paper

**Computer Systems
Associates**
PO Box 129
Jarrettsville, MD 20184-9998
Web site: www.vquilt.com
Vquilt

Connectix Corporation
2955 Campus Drive,
Suite 100
San Mateo, CA 94403
Phone: (800) 950-5880
Web site:
www.connectix.com
*Virtual PC with
Windows 98*

Deneba Software
1150 NW 72nd Avenue
Miami, FL 33126
Phone: (305) 596-5644
Web site: www.deneba.com
Canvas

Electric Quilt Company
419 Gould Street, Suite 2
Bowling Green, OH 43402
Phone: (800) 356-4219
Web site:
www.electricquilt.com
*Electric Quilt 4.1, Sew
Precise!, Blockbase,
STASH*

Golden Threads
2 S. 373 Seneca Drive
Wheaton, IL 60187
Phone: (630) 510-2067
Fax: (630) 510-0491
E-mail: gldnthread@aol.com
Web site:
www.goldenthreads.com
Proportional scale

Irma Gail Hatcher
916 Heather Circle
Conway, AR 72034
E-mail:
jighatcher@cyberback.com
*Hot Fudge Sundae & Irish
Eyes, Plus 10 Secrets of
Quilt Designs*

Just a Little Something
304 Sixth Street SW
Rochester, MN 55902
Phone: (507) 288-7172
E-mail:
quiltsandminis@aol.com
*Crystal Paper foundation
transfer paper*

Mace Motif
106 Manito Road
Manasquan, NJ 08736
Phone: (732) 223-4434
Magic Design mirrors

Nancy's Notions
PO Box 683
333 Beichl Avenue
Beaver Dam, WI 53916
Phone: (800) 833-0690
Web site:
www.nancysnotions.com
Proportional scale

OmniGrid Rulers
Prym-Dritz Corporation
PO Box 5028
Spartanburg, SC 29304
Phone: (800) 845-4948
Web site: www.dritz.com

PCQuilt
75 Sherwood Avenue
Ossining, NY 10562
Phone: (800) 731-8886
Web site: www.pcquilt.com
PCQuilt

Primrose Gradations
PO Box 6
Two Harbors, MN 55616
Phone: (888) 393-2787
Web site: www.dyearts.com
Hand-dyed fabrics

Quilt-Pro Systems, Inc.
PO Box 560692
The Colony, TX 75056
Phone: (800) 884-1511
Web site: www.quiltpro.com
*1-2-3- Quilt! and Quilt-
Pro 3 for Windows and
Macintosh, Foundation
Factory, Block Factory*

QuiltSOFT
PO Box 19946
San Diego, CA 92159-0946
Web site:
www.quiltsoft.com
QuiltSOFT

Index

INDEX